THE BOOK OF
MYSTERIES,
MAGIC
AND THE
UNEXPLAINED

WRITTEN BY
TAMARA MACFARLANE

ILLUSTRATED BY
KRISTINA KISTER

CONTENTS

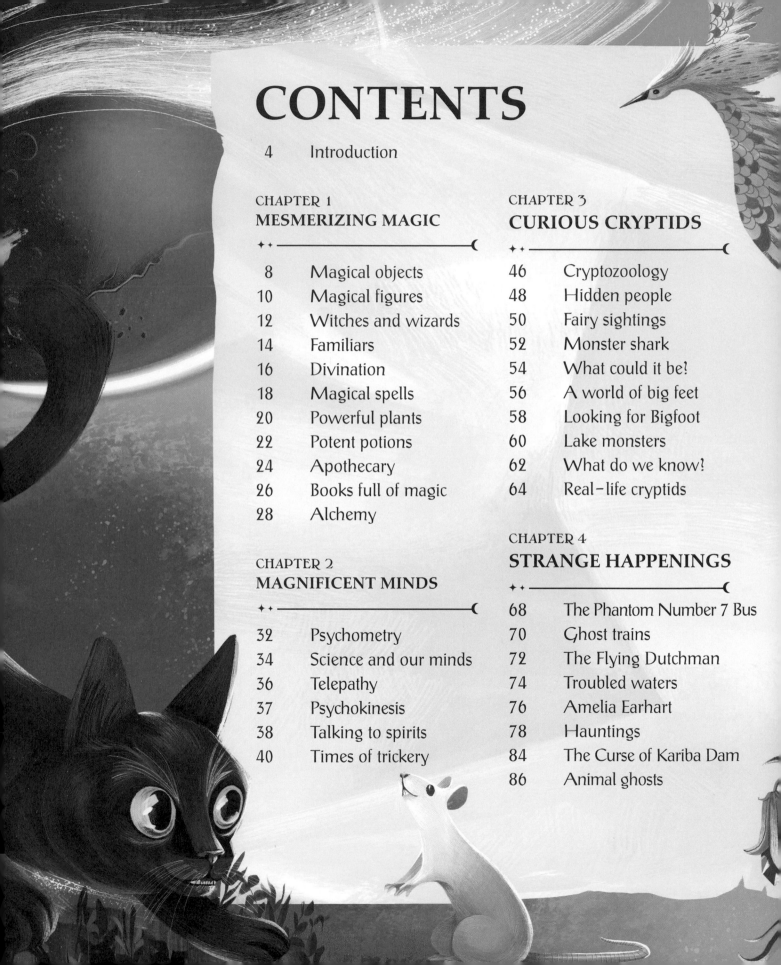

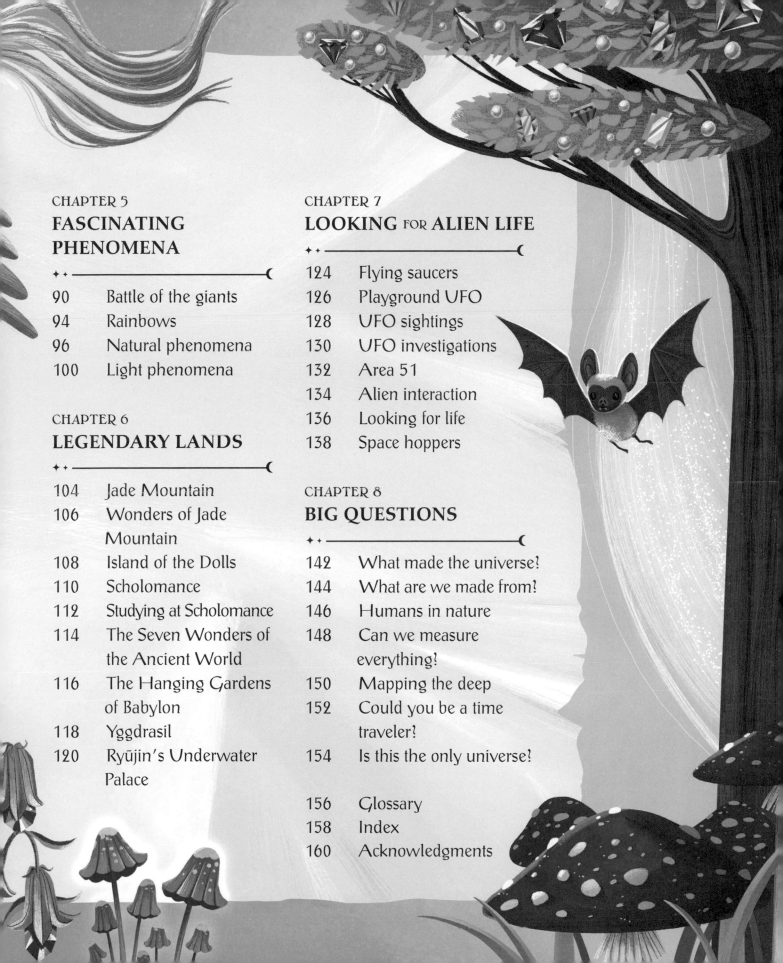

INTRODUCTION

English science fiction writer Arthur C. Clarke once said, "I don't pretend to have all the answers, but the questions are worth thinking about." To question is to wonder, and this book is all about wonder. It wonders about the kind of questions that have answers lurking, just beyond our grasp, around the next corner, or over the next page...

There are so many questions that have puzzled humans for thousands of years that mythology, religion, and science have attempted to explain, which we may never find answers for... but perhaps these are the most interesting questions of all.

So, as you wander across the pages of this book, venturing into the unknown, you may be accompanied by spirits, guided by familiars, or led by alien life. But whatever strangeness you stumble upon, try and keep a sense of wonder, for you do not know what magic and mystery may be waiting...

CHAPTER 1

MESMERIZING MAGIC

Have you ever wished that you had magical powers—that a twitch of your nose could clean your room, a sprinkle of "Abracadabras" would do your homework, or, with a pinch of this and three drops of that, a disgusting meal could become the forbidden feast of your dreams? Magic is everywhere, but what would you do with it if you only had the power?

Magical objects

Witches, wizards, and other makers of magic often need some basic tools to make their magical prowess happen. It's hard to imagine a witch without a cauldron or a wizard without a wand, but there are a lot of other important magical objects, too...

Cauldron

Can you imagine a better object to use for mixing potions and chanting spells! A huge cauldron was found in the Thames River in London, England, in 1861. It is over 3,000 years old and was made in the Iron Age.

Tarot cards

Each one of the 78 cards in a pack of tarot cards is unique, with a different picture and meaning. The tarot reader deals the cards out in a particular pattern. Both the symbol on the card and the position that it is in are important. People may use them to ask for guidance in their lives.

Amulets

An amulet is a charm, often worn as a pendant or necklace. It is believed to protect the wearer by warding off danger and bad luck. Amulets may contain precious stones and be inscribed with magical words and symbols.

Wand

Sort of like a lightning conductor, a wand allows magic-makers to direct the magic from all around them into one place before releasing it. This ensures that the spells work on the people, creatures, and places they are intended for. You don't want to turn the wrong person into a frog by accident!

Crystal balls

People who can see the future are called clairvoyants. They stare into crystal balls to help them tell people's fortunes. An image appears inside the ball, which is said to tell the clairvoyant something about the person who has come to see them. Just as the image is about to appear, it is said to become misty inside the crystal ball.

Crystals

Crystals have a natural beauty, and some people believe they have mysterious powers. For example, jade is thought to bring good fortune, rose quartz to calm the mind, and black tourmaline to offer protection.

Rune stones

Runes can be made from many different materials, including wood, stone, pebbles, crystals, and bone. They have special symbols engraved on them. A person who wants help making a decision would scatter the runes and then interpret the different symbols and where they fall to find the answer.

9

Magical figures

Figures associated with magic were often highly respected and important members of society, the same way doctors and scientists are today. Some ideas and methods from early magical practice have helped shape certain scientific fields, such as medicine and astronomy.

Sangomas

Sangomas are highly respected healers among the Zulu people of South Africa, and they diagnose problems that may be physical, emotional, or spiritual. They may use bones or other objects to help them to divine what is wrong with the patient. Sangomas then perform rituals and create herbal medicines to treat their patients.

Oracles

Oracles are magic-users who can see the future. In Ancient Greece, people believed that the gods spoke directly through oracles. One of the most famous oracles was the Oracle of Delphi, who was a priestess. Many people traveled to Delphi to seek advice or guidance from her.

Shamans

A shaman travels to the spirit world and asks the spirits for guidance on things like how to heal sickness or how to predict the future. In some cultures, a shaman consults the spirits for direction or advice if their community has any major questions that need answering.

While shamans commune with the spirit world, astrologers use stars and planets to predict the future.

Astrologers

Stars and planets are in a constant dance across the sky, lining up in certain ways and forming patterns (called constellations). Astrologers use the stars and constellations to gain information and predict the future.

Witches and wizards

Legendary figures who deal in magic, with good or evil intent...

If you think for a moment about how you imagine a witch, it might be a green and warty aged woman, hunched over a bubbling cauldron, about to work evil magic. If you think about how you imagine a wizard, it might be a wise old man, with a long, white beard, working on spells to solve problems. Why do we have such different ideas about the women and men who practice magic? Why are female workers of magic often shown as dark and evil, while male ones are shown as wise and worthy?

It is an interesting question to think about, as most magical practice is the same, whatever the gender of the practitioner. It would usually involve spell-craft: gathering plants and other ingredients, performing rituals, chanting spells, and creating potions, in order to create a change in the physical world.

The potions came in different forms. Some could be drunk, and others were used as lotions and salves. These potions would often involve plants and ingredients with medicinal properties, and would be given to the townspeople to ward off illness.

Some witches and wizards believed in gods, while others did not. For those who did believe in gods, sometimes their spells would involve objects that were seen to be important to the particular god that they were asking for help.

A coven is a group of magic practitioners. While an individual witch or wizard can be very powerful, it is believed that whole groups make spells even more potent.

Familiars

Cats

Sharp-eyed, watchful, and patient, cats were worshiped by the ancient Egyptians, who believed that they were gods with mystical powers. It is said that cats choose their own masters. Intelligent, intuitive, fiercely independent, and all-seeing, cats make ideal companions. Just remember that you belong to them and not the other way around.

Rats

Unlike cats, rats are not thought to have magical powers, but there are other reasons they are a good choice as a familiar. Being so small, rats are able to squeeze into the tiniest spaces, making them excellent spies for their masters. Most importantly though, like cats, they are deeply loyal and protective by nature.

Most witches and wizards have a familiar by their side. Fiercely loyal companions, familiars are spirit creatures who often take the form of small animals. They are there to protect, serve, or guide their magical guardian.

Bats

Appearing at night and in the shadows, bats have long been considered mystical creatures. Unfortunately for the bat, it is their blood and other body parts that are thought to contain the real magic. Some cultures even believed that bathing your eyes in bat's blood would give you the power to become invisible.

Owls

Owls are believed to act as psychic spies, weave protective magic, and deliver vital messages. They can even strengthen their owner's magic and may share their mysticism and wisdom with their wizard or witch just by being near them.

Divination

Divination is a type of magic that uses objects, symbols, and signs to help answer questions or see into the future. This includes "reading" tea leaves to see what patterns they make in a cup, or gazing into a crystal ball. There are hundreds of different types of divinations, from reading the weather to interpreting our dreams.

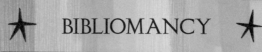
BIBLIOMANCY

Bibliomancy is the art of divining using books. You can take any book and let it fall open at a page. Something on that page will help you to answer a particular question.

PALMISTRY

In palmistry, a skilled palm reader looks at a person's hands and "reads" particular lines on their hands to find out a person's characteristics and to predict future events.

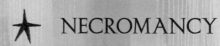
NECROMANCY

A necromancer uses witchcraft or sorcery to waken spirits or to communicate with the dead in order to get information from beyond this earthly realm.

AEROMANCY

Have you ever looked up at the clouds and noticed the different shapes they make! In aeromancy, different weather patterns are read for signs of what might be to come.

CATOPTROMANCY

Imagine the wicked stepmother's mirror in *Snow White* or the Wicked Witch of the West's crystal ball in *The Wizard of Oz.* Catoptromancy is using mirrors to read signs, while crystallomancy uses crystals.

ONEIROMANCY

Some people believe that our dreams carry messages and can help us to make sense of our experiences. The art of interpreting dreams is called oneiromancy.

CARTOMANCY

A cartomancer uses cards, such as playing or tarot, to read the future. Each card in the deck has a different meaning, as does the order in which the cards are dealt.

Magical spells

Spells can be used to do good or to cause harm. That choice is in the hands of the spell-maker. Spells come in many different forms and have a rich and varied history. Here are just some of the most well-known spells in history.

Abracadabra

In the 2nd century CE, "Abracadabra" was recorded in a medical textbook by Serenus Sammonicus, a Roman doctor and tutor. In his book, Sammonicus wrote ABRACADABRA in a triangle shape by removing the last letter on every line. It was believed that by wearing this triangle of letters on an amulet or pendant, you would be protected from deadly diseases.

ABRACADABRA
ABRACADABR
ABRACADAB
ABRACADA
ABRACAD
ABRACA
ABRAC
ABRA
ABR
AB
A

Curses

In ancient Greek and Roman times, if somebody disrespected you or caused you harm, you could pay someone to curse them for you by writing on a curse tablet. These tablets were made of lead, wax, or stone, and had spells etched onto them.

Invisibility spell

Have you ever wished that you could become invisible! Luckily, there is a spell for this in a text known as *The Key of Knowledge*. It is believed to have been the grimoire (book of spells) of the biblical King Solomon. All you needed to do was to chant the set of words shown on the right and you would become invisible!

Stabbon, Asen, Gabellum, Saneney, Noty, Enobal, Labonerem, Balametem, Balnon, Tygumel, Millegaly, Juneneis, Hearma, Hamorache, Yesa, Seya, Senoy, Henen, Barucatha, Acararas, Taracub, Bucarat, Caramy, by the mercy whitch you beare towardes mann kynde, make me to be invysible.

Love spells

Love spells often have titles that give a clue about what they do. A "fetching" love spell is intended to bring the object of love to the person performing the magic. When performing these spells, it was important to include the time, date, and location in which the object of love should arrive. Leaving out these details could mean people being magicked up to the wrong place at the wrong time!

The Tree of Knowledge

The Tree of Knowledge is an ancient Hebrew book containing 125 spells for many purposes, including healing, love, protection, and curses. There is even one to help you catch thieves. The spell instructs the user to write some key words on parchment and tie this around a black rooster's neck. The rooster then circles the suspects until it jumps onto the head of the guilty person!

Powerful plants

Humans need plants. We need them to keep us alive. They feed us, keep us warm, give us shelter, and clean the air that we breathe. We even use them as medicines to heal us.

Rosemary was believed to banish witches and was planted near gates and doors.

Mugwort was used in oil, and put onto the skin to ease aching muscles.

Sage was an important herb in medicine and cleansing, and is still used today.

In ancient Roman times, crowns of mint were believed to enhance memory.

Hundreds of years ago, it was not easy to get help if you were sick or injured. Doctors were difficult to find, and it was costly to get treatment. Instead, people turned to nature and used specific plants, herbs, and flowers to help them recover. Healers and spiritual workers used their knowledge of these plants to create special remedies to treat illness and are considered early examples of apothecaries. Using their knowledge and skills, they would prepare medicines from the plants that grew nearby.

Some medicines used today were originally developed from plants. Take aspirin, a commonly used painkiller—its active ingredient is acetylsalicylic acid, which is found in the bark of the white willow tree. For centuries, people used white willow bark to help ease pain and inflammation—and it's still used today as a tea, or a compress.

But magic workers didn't just use plants for their medicinal qualities. Plants were also used in spells, as they were believed to have magical as well as healing powers.

Lavender is a natural antiseptic and is believed to have calming properties.

Mistletoe

Mistletoe is popular at Christmas, and it features in a Norse myth. Balder was the son of Frigg, the goddess of love. She asked every plant and animal to promise they would never harm her beloved son. But she forgot to ask the mistletoe. The mischievous god Loki found out about her mistake. He made an arrow from the mistletoe and shot Balder with it.

Plants as incense

Plants are still used today in sacred places, such as churches and temples. Using smoke to cleanse a space is practiced in cultures across the world. Different herbs are collected and dried out. They are either set on fire or placed onto hot coals. The smoke from the burning plants is fragrant and is believed to ward off evil spirits.

Plants as poison

Some plants are poisonous. Even plants used as medicine can be dangerous if the dose is too large. There is a garden in Northumberland, England, called the Poison Garden, where you can learn about poisonous plants. Visitors are instructed not to touch, taste, or even smell the plants.

Curing nightmares

Medieval monks grew the ingredients to make potions for a lot of different ailments. One potion that they made was to cure nightmares. Peony seeds were soaked in wine to create a healing bedtime drink.

Poisonous potions

Did you know that witches may have applied potions to their brooms to make them fly! These potions had poisonous ingredients such as belladonna (deadly nightshade) and hemlock. It is now known that many of these poisonous ingredients can affect the human brain in strange ways, creating hallucinations—so perhaps they led witches to think that they could fly!

Potent potions

Bubbling, spitting, fizzing and frothing, from witches' brews to fairy foam, magic potions come in wildly colored concoctions and have many different uses. Whether it's a poultice to heal a donkey's hoof, a lotion to make you float, or a boiling syrup to turn the class bully into a frog, there is no end to the potency of potions.

Creating a potion

A true potion-maker needs to be skilled at combining the right ingredients in very exact amounts to achieve the best possible results. This takes years of practice and endless experimentation in order to perfect the most effective potions.

Love potion

Love potion recipes have been passed down from the Middle Ages. A popular one involved mixing earthworms with powdered periwinkle plant and mixed herbs. Once mashed together, the concoction was either eaten by the couple or spread onto the chest of the person who was admired.

CRUSH TOGETHER:
1 EARTHWORM
1 PORTION OF POWDERED PERIWINKLE
1 PORTION OF MIXED HERBS

Don't try these at home!

Eye of newt

Witches sometimes used secret codes in their potions. If I said that you had "eye of newt" in your burger, you would probably be disgusted! But eye of newt was actually a witch's code for mustard seed. So if you order a burger, there might be a few eyes of newts in there!

A potion-making class

One of the early textbooks was a natural history encyclopedia called *Ortus Sanitatis*, or *The Garden of Health*. It is illustrated and shows a picture of students and their teacher having a lesson on potion-making.

Apothecary

The early makers of medicine were called apothecaries, and they mixed their medicinal cures in an apothecary shop.

Overflowing with jars of extraordinary ingredients, apothecary shops sound like magical places to us today. Although apothecaries used many strange ingredients that seem as though they belong in a potion rather than a medicine, apothecaries were actually early medical scientists, meticulously developing treatments for their patients.

An apothecary was a place where dragon's blood, boar's grease, and bear fat nestled on shelves next to liquorice, sage, willow, and rose petals. Apothecaries also needed a lot of equipment to measure and mix their healing treatments. Weighing scales, a pestle and mortar to grind up herbs, and various tools for heating and cooling ingredients were used.

Strange as it might be, many of our modern medicines have their origins in nature. Healing properties found in plants and fungi, mold, and even insects have been used throughout human history. In fact, some of the cures that they were using in apothecaries hundreds of years ago are still used in medicine today.

So-called dragon's blood isn't really blood at all but a bright red plant resin. It has been used as medicine since ancient times, and it is still in use today.

CAPSICUM ANNUUM

CHAMOMILA

BRYOPHYTA

BROMINE

Books full of magic

Some of the oldest historical writings that have been discovered, from across many different cultures, are about magic spells and rituals. Books of magic come in different forms—some are full of useful and practical information, while others are filled with spells that were considered so evil that the books were made illegal and banned or burned!

Grimoire

A grimoire is a book that helps with magical knowledge, such as instructions on rituals and spell ingredients. A grimoire might also be used to look up the significance of particular colors, meanings of crystals, uses for plants, and more.

Book of Shadows

A Book of Shadows is a magic-maker's personal journal. They fill it with their own spells and potion recipes, and use it to keep a record of their experiments and findings. These journals are not for sharing and are best kept in a secret place to stop others from stealing their precious discoveries.

Books of the Dead

These ancient Egyptian collections of spells, prayers, advice, and maps were usually written on papyrus leaves and then placed in the burial chambers of people who had died. The books contained 165 spells along with other information that the ancient Egyptians believed would help guide the deceased's spirit on its journey into the afterlife.

The Key of Solomon

The Key of Solomon is an example of a medieval grimoire. It is divided into two books, and contains information and instructions on how to summon demons and spirits of the dead. Also included are ingredients you might need to make ink for drawing magic symbols, what to wear when chanting, and a guide to creating curses for managing any disobedient demons.

The Picatrix

One of the most important works of medieval magic, the *Picatrix* is a handbook for mixing magical compounds, summoning planetary spirits, and figuring out astrological conditions. It is over 400 pages long, and the information inside it was collected from magic practice across Egypt, India, Persia, and the Middle East.

Alchemy

Alchemists were early scientists, exploring strange substances and performing daring experiments.

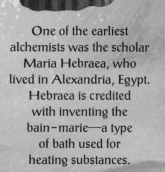

One of the earliest alchemists was the scholar Maria Hebraea, who lived in Alexandria, Egypt. Hebraea is credited with inventing the bain-marie—a type of bath used for heating substances.

The philosopher's stone may not have been a stone at all. It has also been described as a powder, a liquid, and an ointment.

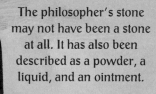

It started with a single question, a question so extraordinary that it flew across continents, fascinating thinkers in different cultures. It sparked 2,000 years of philosophical thought and formed the beginnings of scientific investigations and processes. All this, from just one idea—the possibility that a single magical ingredient might exist, an ingredient so powerful that it could turn any metal into gold, cure the human body of every illness, and cleanse the human spirit to make it immortal.

Early alchemists were greatly influenced by an Arabic text called the *Emerald Tablet.* They became focused on finding a single magical ingredient that became known as the philosopher's stone. So a global treasure hunt started that involved looking for clues in the stars, solving puzzles, experimenting, and challenging traditional ideas. This search began in Egypt, China, and India, and the ideas spread out to many parts of the world.

Alchemists hid their findings in coded text and shrouded their experiments in secrecy. Perhaps the real treasure at the end of the great alchemic hunt was the beginning of science in all its forms— biology, chemistry, and physics—leading ultimately to the founding of modern medicine and its ability to cure illness. And so, in a sense, the philosopher's stone could be said to be not a stone, powder, or ointment, but to be the earthly power of human exploration and knowledge.

Early alchemists believed that everything came from four elements: fire, water, air, and earth. These elements are represented by a triangle containing a square within a circle on the symbol for the philosopher's stone below...

The part of the symbol combining the four elements of fire, water, air, and earth is known as the squared circle. The larger, outer circle, created by a dragon or serpent swallowing its own tail, symbolizes the complete circle of life and the idea of infinity. This part of the symbol is known as the Ouroboros.

29

CHAPTER 2

MAGNIFICENT MINDS

Our minds are truly magnificent things, capable of making sense of the real world, while our imaginations conjure up extraordinary things, dream the impossible, and explore the unknown. Our minds allow us to choose to tell the truth or to trick others, to look for evidence or to simply believe. Complex, complicated, and intelligent enough to read this sentence, have you ever really thought about how your mind works?

Psychometry

Psychometry is the ability to discover facts about an event or person by touching objects that are associated with them. People who can sense information from objects are said to be "psychic."

Believing that inanimate objects contain a soul or a spirit is called animism and dates back to early humans. While over time, science and religion have changed beliefs around this, the idea that objects could still hold a vital essence has survived. Even today, some people believe that objects can pick up energy from people or events around them.

Psychometry is the practice of tapping into or reading these energies. The term "psychometry" comes from the Greek "psyche," meaning spirit, and

Psychic helpers

There have been many fake psychics and mediums, often taking advantage of people grieving loved ones. This has meant that the idea of using psychics to help solve mysteries is largely discredited. While police forces are unlikely to talk openly about receiving psychic help to solve a crime, there are a number of cases where the use of help from a psychic has been made public.

"metron," meaning to measure. It was coined in the 19th century by Joseph Buchanan, a professor of physiology.

One example of psychometry is its use in police and criminal investigations. Although there is a lot of discussion around their actual effectiveness, psychics have used psychometry to help police with investigations into missing people as well as other unsolved cases.

It is believed that by holding onto possessions of a lost or dead person, the energies stored within the object can help provide information about the person's last movements. One such psychic was Gerard Croiset. After Croiset provided Dutch police with information that led to a conviction, he assisted in missing persons and murder cases—though the results were mixed.

TOP
SE(RE

Without doubt, fraudulent practice has led to the discrediting of many psychics. However, we still know so little about how our mind works that perhaps as studies of the brain develop we'll find there is more potential than we realize...

Arizona's district attorney's office is reported to have been helped in their investigations by a psychic named Allison DuBois. Most of her information came to her in dreams.

CASE CLOSED

Science and our minds

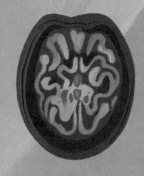

Using scans, we can watch particular areas of the brain light up during different activities, but we don't yet know how the brain processes information.

Our brains are completely miraculous. Just think about how much information is being fed into them every second...

All of our five basic senses—touch, taste, smell, hearing, and sight—are constantly sending information to our brains, helping us to understand the world around us. As well as these five main senses, we also have other less well-known ones, including spatial awareness and balance.

Our unconcious mind is constantly processing information that we are not even aware of. Have you ever been talking to a friend next to you and then heard your name in a different conversation right across the room? Your conscious mind was listening to your friend, but your nonconscious mind was also hearing everything else going on around you.

Is it possible that some of the things that we think of as being psychic can be explained by the huge amount of information that our brains are processing without us even realizing!

While many people believe that they, or other people, have psychic powers, scientific studies are still inconclusive. However, we are discovering many new things about our brains, including learning about other senses, so that as brain science develops, there will be many more amazing discoveries to be made. Nobody knows what the future of brain science will hold...

Telepathy

Telepathy is the ability to communicate with others by thought, instead of through our known senses.

Have you ever felt as though you knew what someone was going to say just before they said it? Or found your dog waiting at the door with a ball in its mouth, just before you'd even stood up to take them to the park!

Many people have had an experience that felt telepathic. In fact, some governments have been so concerned about people using telepathy to steal state secrets that they have set up projects to investigate. In 1978, at Fort Meade in Maryland, the military began a program called the Stargate Project to look into telepathy. However, the results proved so mixed that it was closed down in 1995.

As with other psychic abilities, it may be that we don't yet understand how what appears to be telepathy works, or how to test for it.

Psychokinesis

Psychokinesis is the ability to move or interact with something physical just by thinking about it.

There are many different forms of psychokinesis. The best known is telekinesis, which is the ability to move objects with thoughts alone. Some other forms of psychokinesis include:

★ Using your mind to make objects change shape—for example, bending a metal spoon or melting a plastic ruler.

★ Changing an object from one form to another.

★ Teleportation—the power to disappear from one place and reappear somewhere else.

★ Creating your own energy field.

★ Using your mind to change a magnetic force.

What would you choose to do if you had the power of psychokinesis!

Talking to spirits

When we talk of a spirit, we usually mean that part of a being that is nonmaterial—it does not exist in any physical form. Some people believe that the spirit lives on in another realm after the body's death.

Spiritualism

Spiritualists believe that there is both a physical and a spiritual realm, and that we are made up of both physical matter and spirit. Spiritualists may communicate with the spirits of the dead through a medium, often at meetings called séances.

Clairvoyance

A clairvoyant is someone who can see into the future or perceive a world beyond the senses and their immediate experience. As such, they can be said to have extrasensory perception (ESP), or a "sixth sense." This knowledge may appear as voices, in dreams, as a thought or feeling, or in a vision.

Mediums

A medium acts as a communication channel between the living people and the spirits of the dead. Some mediums may bring comfort to those who have lost loved ones, while others have been found to be fake, making up messages for money. The three Fox sisters of New York were popular mediums of the 1800s, but their "communications" with spirits turned out to be hoaxes.

Séances

At a séance, a medium communicates with the spirits of those who are no longer living. These meetings would usually be attended by one medium and a number of people wanting to receive messages from dead loved ones.

Times of trickery

In the 1800s, some people realized that they could make a lot of money by pretending to be mediums—a type of psychic able to talk to spirits. These "psychics" tricked desperate people into believing that their dead relatives were really communicating with them at events called séances.

Ectoplasm

Ectoplasm was a mysterious substance that was believed to be produced by a medium when they were in a trance. The substance was said to form itself into the shape of the spirit that the medium was communicating with. To create the illusion of ectoplasm, fake mediums used everything from smoke to white sheets coming out of their mouths.

Hearing voices

In the 1800s, there were many scientific and technological advances made, and some of these seemed as mystical as the ability to talk to spirits. Speeding trains, disembodied voices on telephones, and instant communication on telegraph wires all developed at this time. So, would belief in hearing the voices of spirits be so outlandish!

Rapping and knocking

Spirit rapping means communicating with people in séances through knocks on walls or furniture. Spirits could confirm their presence with a knock or even spell out messages. The Fox sisters were mediums from the state of New York, who used a system of apples on strings, and later their own knuckles and joints, to make rapping sounds.

Suspicious photography

The interest in communicating with spirits through mediums happened in Europe and North America at around the same time that photography was invented. Because photography was new, most people were unaware of how it worked, and it was easy to fool them into believing that fake photographs of levitating tables, disembodied humans, and ghosts were all real.

Table-raising

Mediums at fake séances used a wide range of tricks of the kind that are performed by magicians today. Getting tables to levitate was one popular trick, and it usually involved the use of a carefully prepared mechanical device to lift the table, rather than a spirit...

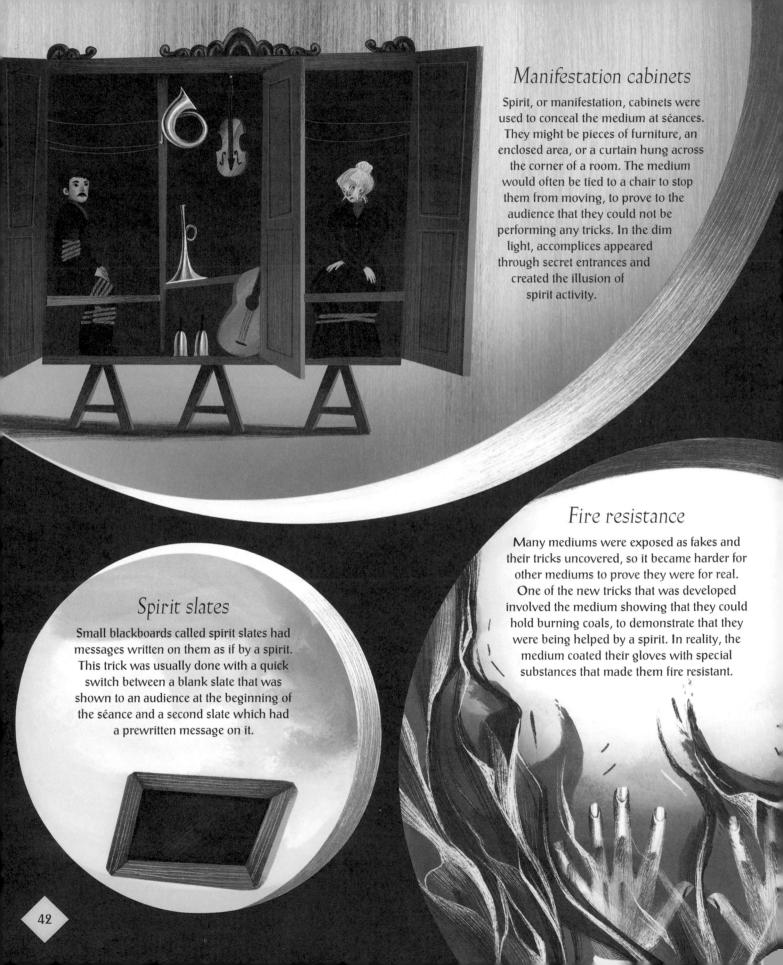

Manifestation cabinets

Spirit, or manifestation, cabinets were used to conceal the medium at séances. They might be pieces of furniture, an enclosed area, or a curtain hung across the corner of a room. The medium would often be tied to a chair to stop them from moving, to prove to the audience that they could not be performing any tricks. In the dim light, accomplices appeared through secret entrances and created the illusion of spirit activity.

Spirit slates

Small blackboards called spirit slates had messages written on them as if by a spirit. This trick was usually done with a quick switch between a blank slate that was shown to an audience at the beginning of the séance and a second slate which had a prewritten message on it.

Fire resistance

Many mediums were exposed as fakes and their tricks uncovered, so it became harder for other mediums to prove they were for real. One of the new tricks that was developed involved the medium showing that they could hold burning coals, to demonstrate that they were being helped by a spirit. In reality, the medium coated their gloves with special substances that made them fire resistant.

Fairies

Elsie and Frances were two young cousins from Yorkshire, England, who tricked a generation of adults into believing that they had taken photos of fairies at the bottom of their garden. Many people were taken in by the Cottingley Fairies, as they became known. The cousins stayed quiet about how they made the photographs for over 60 years before Elsie admitted that they had in fact used cut-out fairy figures.

The human mind has an extraordinary ability to make sense of the world around us, but it can be easily tricked, too. Magicians appear to be able to make the impossible happen. But unlike the fake mediums of the Victorian era, magicians are clear that they are using trickery to do this. The art is in the skill of creating an illusion. Many people love watching magicians performing magic tricks, even though they know that what they are seeing isn't real.

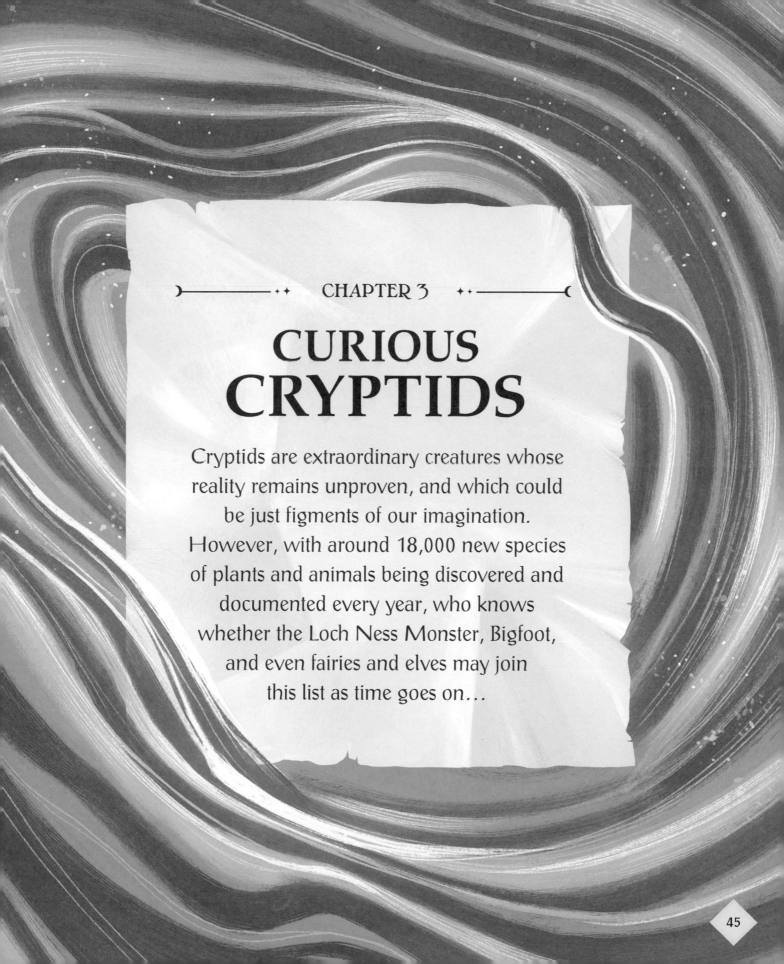

CHAPTER 3

CURIOUS CRYPTIDS

Cryptids are extraordinary creatures whose reality remains unproven, and which could be just figments of our imagination. However, with around 18,000 new species of plants and animals being discovered and documented every year, who knows whether the Loch Ness Monster, Bigfoot, and even fairies and elves may join this list as time goes on…

Cryptozoology

Cryptozoology is the study of legendary or extinct animals. While not thought of as a real science, it is linked to the sciences of zoology and paleontology. Here are some of the types of creatures, called cryptids, that cryptozoologists study.

Hoax

People have been known to create a new creature as a hoax, which is a trick that is intended to deceive. Take the Fiji mermaid, for example—here the head of a monkey was sewn onto the body of a fish to create a mermaid–like creature. It was believed to be real at first, but was later declared to be a hoax.

The Fiji mermaid

Unconfirmed

There are some cryptids that a few people think may be real, but sightings have not been confirmed, nor scientific evidence found to prove their existence. The giant dragonfish, for example, has apparently been sighted just once, off the island of Bermuda. It was said to look like a dragonfish, only much bigger.

Giant dragonfish

Proposed

The "proposed" category of cryptids contains legendary creatures that have an alternative scientific explanation. For instance, the most likely reason for recorded sightings of the kraken of Norse mythology is that it was actually the very real giant squid or collosal squid that was being observed at the time.

Kraken

Extinct

This category refers to real animals that are now considered to be extinct, but which cryptozoologists believe may have living relatives. One example of this is the Loch Ness Monster of Scottish folklore, who it's claimed may be a living relative of the prehistoric plesiosaur.

Plesiosaur

Confirmed

While many creatures studied by cryptozoologists probably don't exist, there are plenty of examples of very strange cryptids that turned out to be living, breathing animals. The okapi, for example, was originally considered to be legendary, but we now know it lives in the rainforests of central Africa.

Okapi

Hidden people

Also known as the little people, fairies, elves, goblins, and pixies flit in and out of legends, fairy tales, and folklore across the world. They appear in many forms, and are capable of both kindness and mischief.

Fairies

Stories about fairies are told around the world. These magical flying creatures may appear as energy or light, or take on a small, humanlike form. Fairies can be good or evil, and are found in both gardens and forests. Their powers depend on the type, with good fairies giving charms and warnings to keep humans safe.

Elves

Appearing first in Nordic folklore, elves come from, and live in, nature. They can talk to animals and plants, and have natural healing powers. Although elves have some human characteristics, they generally prefer to avoid humans. They are great at craftwork—making things that human hands aren't capable of.

Goblins

These little troublemakers are the naughtiest of all the hidden people. Sneaking around in western European folklore, goblins have been known to steal nightclothes off sleeping people, and bang pots and pans around in the night. They are similar to the *tengu*—Japanese monster-spirits who cause fires and eat children, so it is said!

Pixies

Popping up in English folklore, these tiny, green-clothed, mischievous creatures can be found dancing under the moonlight in woodland clearings to the music of bees and butterflies. Their other favorite pastimes include anything naughty that they can think of, including blowing out candles and sending travelers in the wrong direction.

49

Fairy sightings

Fairies are favorite characters in many myths,
but do they have any basis in reality?

Could these tiny, winged creatures be
real fairies, or is it just a trick of the eye!

Fairy photographs

In 1917, two young cousins snapped
photos that appeared to show fairies in
their garden in Cottingley, England.
Many people, including the writer
Arthur Conan Doyle, were fooled, but it
turned out the images were fakes made
using cardboard cutouts. Others have
tried to capture fairies on camera, too, but
none have been proven authentic... yet.

Mistaken identity

Often, the most likely explanation for
a reported fairy sighting is a simple
case of mistaken identity. Although
fairies in myths and legends come in
all shapes and sizes, we tend to think
of them as being very small, with
delicate wings. This means that, at a
glance, a number of insects may look
similar to fairies.

Related to aphids,
aptly named fairy
flies are covered in
white wax, which
helps them to drift
on the wind.

With their feathery
white wings, white
plume moths have an
angelic, fairylike
appearance.

Spirits or ghosts

Some people have suggested that fairies do exist and that they are from another realm. Arthur Conan Doyle was particularly interested in the Cottingley Fairies photographs, partly because he was a spiritualist. His curiosity about the spirit realm extended to fairylike ghosts and spirits, which he believed appeared on Earth, but are not of the Earth.

Power of the imagination
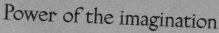

Writers and artists have created wonderful images of fairies throughout the ages. We can get so caught up in the many great stories that it is easy to feel that fairies are real—and in a sense, they are—they live and breathe as they dance across our imaginations!

Could it be that sightings are rare because fairies are so good at playing hide-and-seek with humans? While people have left their mark on much of the land in the world, there are still plenty of unspoiled areas to be explored. Perhaps there are fairies hiding out in these remote places, where nature has remained untouched!

Monster shark

Over a hundred years ago, an impossibly gigantic, mysterious shark was spotted by a group of fishermen... What could it have been?

Imagine a fin taller than a person swerving its way through the water. Now, imagine what else lies below the water's surface and how truly colossal this creature must be. Could it be a monster shark, like the one described by fishermen off the coast of Australia in 1918 as being "ghostly white" and measuring over 98 ft (30 m) long!

Over the years, there have been many reported sightings of impossibly large sharks, often by experienced fishermen who are familiar with marine life. These extraordinary creatures have made their way into stories, but is there any evidence for their existence?

As with many of the creatures studied by cryptozoologists, the monster shark closely resembles a real creature, the megalodon, a giant prehistoric shark with 276 serrated teeth, each one the size of an adult human hand. Fossil remains show that its jaws were so big that it could swallow a person whole!

However, it is commonly accepted by scientific evidence that the megalodon became extinct around 3.5 million years ago. So, what could possibly explain these modern-day sightings?

A fossilized megalodon tooth compared to a great white shark tooth— there's little doubt which is bigger!

What could it be?

Most of the world's oceans remain unexplored, leaving endless possibilities as to what might be living there. Here are some possible suspects that might explain the sighting of the monster shark.

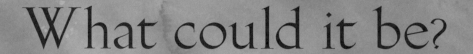

Outsized great white shark

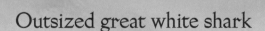

Megamouth shark

Outsized great white shark

Every now and then, a particularly large version of an animal or marine creature can appear. These are very rare within each species, but there are many examples across the animal kingdom. The largest shark on record, a female known as Deep Blue, measures over 20 ft (6 m) long.

Megamouth shark

This deepwater shark is rarely seen by humans. It was only discovered in 1976, and since then, fewer than 100 have ever been spotted. It is a smaller relative of the whale shark and is harmless to humans, but its giant mouth may have led to stories of extraordinary, outsized sea beasts.

Human

Megalodon

Whale shark

Whale shark

This gentle shark is the largest fish in the world. There are examples of the whale shark growing over 59 ft (18 m) long. In Madagascar, the whale shark is known as *marokintana*, which means "many stars," after the patterned markings on the surface of its back.

Megalodon

While we can't be absolutely sure, it is unlikely that a surviving megalodon is the monster shark. Megalodon fossil remains disappear from the fossil record around 3.5 million years ago. If megalodons still exist, it is extremely likely that we would have discovered some evidence of them.

A world of big feet

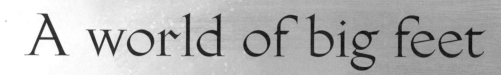

Sightings of giant, hairy, humanlike creatures have been reported from places all around the world, but do they really exist?

Yeti

Found in the icy, snow-covered Himalayan mountains of Asia, the Yeti is probably the best-known type of Bigfoot. Also called the Abominable Snowman, it is fur-covered, muscular, and walks on two feet. Not as tall as you might think, the Yeti is believed to be around 6 ft (1.8 m) in height.

Mapinguari

This giant, sloth-like creature is said to live in the Amazon rainforest in Brazil. The Mapinguari is known for its terrible smell, so bad that it can knock out a human. Some people have claimed that it has a human mouth in the middle of its stomach.

Yeren

Long ago, in the forests of ancient China, a giant, apelike creature called a Yeren was reported to have been seen. The Yeren ranged from 6–10 ft (1.8–3 m) in height and was covered with red fur. The creature was said to be calm and peaceful, and kept well away from any human contact.

Sasquatch

This large and hairy primate is said to live in northwest USA and Canada. The Sasquatch ranges from 6–15 ft (1.8–4.6 m) in height, and its footprints are said to be a whopping 24 in (61 cm) long and over 8 in (20 cm) wide. Not the quietest of creatures, the Sasquatch lets out a high-pitched sound as it moves.

Looking for Bigfoot

Giant mythical creatures like Bigfoot are found in many different cultures around the world. Why might that be?

English mountaineer Eric Shipton took a photograph of a giant footprint in the Himalayan snow in 1951. Could it be the Yeti! Nobody knows...

Mistaken identity

A number of key sightings of these giants of folklore have turned out to be a case of mistaken identity. For example, a sample of hairs said to be from the Yeti was studied and found to belong to the Tibetan blue bear—an endangered animal living in the Himalayan mountains of Asia.

Human imagination

Humans have amazing imaginations. For instance, we may spot one unfamiliar animal, such as the lesula monkey, which has a face a little bit like a hairy human. Our imagination might then fill in gaps in our knowledge so that we might think it is actually a strange–looking man—or a Bigfoot!

New discoveries

We are constantly finding out new things that can change our view of the world. We know that there are animals that used to have giant versions—such as the giant shark megalodon. Very rarely, people might have a large amount of growth hormones in their body and grow to be extremely tall.

In the woods of northern California...

Among other places, there have been reports of sightings of Bigfoot in the forests of western USA. Is it a coincidence that this is also the home of the American black bear!

Around the Great Lakes...

In 1976, research scientists in Ethiopia found remains of a type of human ancestor, later named *Homo bodoensis*, that had not been identified before.

In Gifford Pinchot National Forest, Washington...

The tallest man in recorded history was American Robert Wadlow. He grew to be 8 ft 11 in (2.72 m) tall.

And so...

There is still so much about our world that we don't know—there might be a lot more animals out there we have never seen! As we keep on exploring, we might find more kinds of humanoid animals who have been living out of sight in their natural surroundings, completely undisturbed by humans.

Nessie

The Loch Ness Monster, also known as Nessie, is said to have a long neck and face, flippers, and either one or two humps. The earliest recorded sighting of Nessie was more than 1,500 years ago by a group of people called the Picts from Scotland. One Pict carving, found close to the shores of Loch Ness, shows an unfamiliar creature with a long face, and flippers instead of feet.

Nessie is said to live in a lake called Loch Ness, in Scotland.

Issie

According to legend, Issie was a horse and lived with her foal near Lake Ikeda, in Japan. When her foal was kidnapped by a Samurai warrior, Issie threw herself into the lake in despair and turned into a water monster. In the 1970s, there were reported sightings of a black creature with two lumps, moving across the lake's surface. Could it have been Issie!

Champ gets its name from its home in Lake Champlain—a huge lake that lies across northeastern USA and Canada.

Lake monsters

Many of the world's lakes reach great depths, so it's easy to imagine mysterious monsters lurking in these watery worlds. And at any moment, they might just break through the silvery surface into sight...

Issie's home is said to be Lake Ikeda, Ibusuki, Japan.

Champ

The mythical Champ is said to resemble a large, horned serpent or giant snake. The Abenaki and the Iroquois, who are the Indigenous peoples of Lake Champlain in North America, have long held legends about a large water monster living in the lake.

What do we know?

Some people think that lake monsters exist,
but could there be other explanations?

Mistaken identity

There are so many animals living in our lakes, is it possible that some sightings were not of lake monsters at all, but were actually of whales, pikes, or other huge fish? One of the most likely look-alikes for Champ, for example, is a fish called a garfish, which is known to live in Lake Champlain.

Garfish

Humpback whale

Pike

How big is big?

Theories abound about possible explanations for Nessie. After all, Loch Ness is 23 miles (37 km) long, and is very deep, too, so it would be easy for a monster to hide here. Despite its size, however, scientists think that there aren't enough fish in the lake to feed such a huge creature as Nessie.

In 1987, boats using sonar equipment were even sent out to search the lake for evidence of Nessie. The search proved fruitless...

At its deepest point, Loch Ness measures around 745 ft (227 m). To get an idea of just how deep this is, imagine the Eiffel Tower sinking into the lake...

Prehistoric reptile

One theory to explain the Loch Ness Monster is that it was a plesiosaur, which had a long neck and small head, like many popular images of Nessie. But no evidence of prehistoric creatures has ever been uncovered in Loch Ness. Also, the water of the lake is probably too cold for giant reptiles to live in.

Plesiosaurus was a prehistoric reptile.

However, later discoveries have put the theory of prehistoric animals being alive today back in the spotlight. Coelacanth fish, once presumed extinct, were found off the coast of South Africa in 1938. So if coelacanth fish are alive and well, who is to say that Nessie isn't either?

Coelacanth fish were once thought to be extinct.

Fossils of plesiosaurs have been found.

Scientific find

Scientists once believed that plesiosaurs only lived in salt water, and Loch Ness is a freshwater lake. However, in 2022, fossils of small plesiosaurs were found in a dried up freshwater riverbed in Morocco. This suggests that some species of plesiosaurs once lived in freshwater. Perhaps plesiosaurs still exist, too, and Nessie could be a freshwater-dwelling example!

There is no hard evidence for the legendary Japanese water monster Issie, either. However, there is one theory to explain the sightings. Lake Ikeda, in Japan, is home to giant eels measuring up to 7 ft (2 m) in length. Is it possible that they have been mistaken for a terrifying monster!

Eel

Real-life cryptids

Cryptids are imaginary creatures of fantasy and folklore. However, quite a few "cryptids" have later turned out to be real. Here are just a few real-life animals, whose existence was once doubted by early scientists. If only these scientists had heeded the knowledge of local people—they could have probably informed them straight away that these animals were very real indeed!

Giant squid

Legends of enormous squid, such as the kraken of Norse myth and the Scylla of Ancient Greece, have been told for thousands of years. They used to be thought of in the same way as mermaids and unicorns. Then, in the 1870s, a real giant squid was washed ashore off Newfoundland, Canada.

Komodo dragon

With their massive claws and venomous fangs, Komodo dragons are the largest-known lizards in the world today. However, in 1910, reports of giant "land crocodiles" from an island off the coast of Indonesia were laughed at.

Dingiso

The Moni people of western Indonesia have long revered the Bondegezou as an ancestral spirit. Today, the Bondegezou, also called the Dingiso, is known to be a rare member of the marsupial family living in the mountain forests of New Guinea in Indonesia.

Cuvier's beaked whale

Also called the "Water Owl," the Ziphius was a creature of medieval folklore. It had the head of an owl and the body of a fish, topped off with a fin that was so sharp it could pierce the hulls of ships. Today, it is better known as the very real Cuvier's beaked whale.

Oarfish

Tales of colossal sea serpents have poured from the mouths of sailors for centuries. There are a number of misidentified sea creatures that could account for the sightings, but the most likely is the oarfish. They have been known to grow up to 98 ft (30 m) long.

Platypus

Scientists considered the platypus to be a hoax when they were first shown this strange animal. An egg-laying mammal with a beaver's tail, a duck's beak, and a venomous spur, the platypus seemed too strange to be true. However, we know now that the platypus is real.

Kangaroo

Thousands of years ago, the Indigenous people of Australia made rock carvings of the kangaroo. In the 1700s, European explorers of Australia told of strange, upright creatures who hopped like frogs. Scientists dismissed these descriptions as fantasy at first.

Mountain gorilla

Fewer than 400 mountain gorillas are thought to be living in the wild today. Like most endangered species, their existence is threatened by human activity. Originally thought to be mythical monsters of the mountains, these plant-eaters are generally quite gentle.

Spot-bellied eagle owl

Sri Lankan folklore tells of a frightening horned bird whose screeches sounded like terrifying screams. For centuries, this bird was heard, but not really seen, until in 2001 it was recorded as a newly discovered type of owl called a spot-bellied eagle owl.

CHAPTER 4

STRANGE HAPPENINGS

What just sent a shiver down your spine! Was it simply a draft from the window, perhaps, or a whisper of something more sinister! Sometimes it might just be a strange feeling, but other times it could be something more…a flickering light, a haunting bark, a spectral figure, a shadow of a thing that isn't actually there…

The Phantom Number 7 Bus

A ghostly bus causes havoc on the streets of London...

In London, England, from the 1930s until 1990, there were a large number of recorded sightings of a spooky, red number 7 double-decker bus careening wildly around a corner into a street named Cambridge Gardens in the middle of the night.

While most witnesses lived to tell the tale, one unfortunate driver died in 1934 when he swerved to avoid crashing into what became known as the Phantom Number 7 Bus. Missing the eerie vehicle, his car exploded into flames when it hit a tree.

The Number 7 bus always appeared around Cambridge Gardens at 1:15 a.m.—a time no buses should have been in the area.

Sightings always reported the bus as driving into the street, completely empty of passengers and with no one in the driver's seat, before speeding down the middle of the road and completely disappearing into the night.

There were so many crashes in this particular spot, and so many individual witnesses to the mysterious appearances of the double-decker, that the police began to investigate. They knew they could not ignore reports from such a large number of people, as they couldn't all have been mistaken.

After interrogating the eyewitnesses, the police began to observe the location for any signs of the phantom bus. While they were unable to confirm the ghostly bus's existence, they decided to improve the lighting and safety in the square by widening the road. The strange sightings then stopped—and yet the mystery remains unsolved.

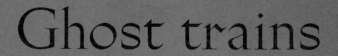

Ghost trains

There are many different ways to travel, but the strangest of them all might be to hop aboard a train that may not really be there...

A silent band is said to play to the ghostly funeral train as it travels along.

Those unlucky enough to board the Silverpilen subway train to Kymlinge station are said never to be seen again—it is the only station with no way out.

70

Abraham Lincoln's funeral train

In 1865, on a moody, misty, Washington, DC, morning, the funeral train of Abraham Lincoln pulled slowly out of the station. The assassination of the country's beloved president had left the nation in grief, and people lined up across the land to see the train carrying his coffin pass by.

Strangely, each year since, there have been reports of the funeral train drifting eerily along the same route. Through the streaming smoke from its engine, witnesses say they can clearly see a group of skeleton soldiers keeping a ghostly guard over the president's body.

The smoke billowing out of the mysterious train is said to be a thick ghoulish green, cloaking the black carriages as it passes through towns and cities. Local clocks ran six minutes fast after the ghost train had slid past.

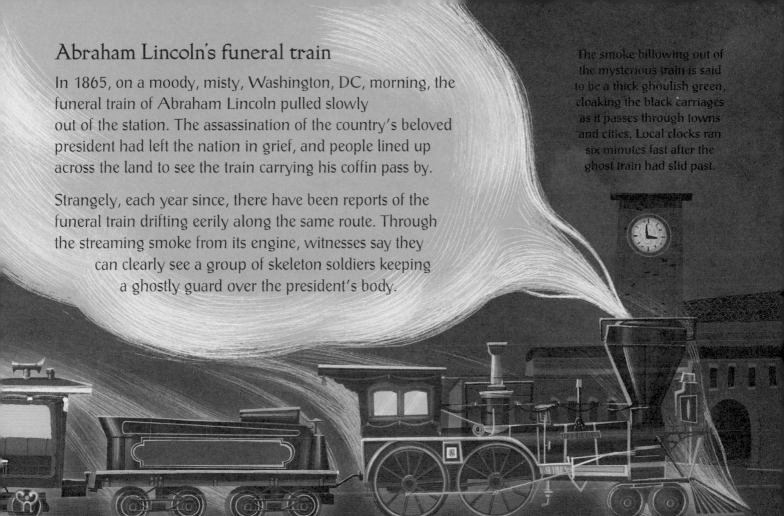

Silverpilen subway train

In Sweden, it is said the spooky Silverpilen subway train travels along Stockholm's underground tracks late at night. It is heading for the decomissioned Kymlinge station, said to be the subway station of the dead, stopping occasionally at random stations. If you happened to be standing on a poorly lit platform somewhere along this train's route, you may not notice its strange, unfinished silver exterior. As you step into one of its carriages, the faces of the other phantom passengers would warn you, too late, that this wasn't your usual train home...

The Silverpilen subway train appears silver, as it is missing its final coat of paint. This is a warning sign that tells you not to get on board!

The Flying Dutchman

Of all the legends of phantom ships, the story of the Flying Dutchman might be the most terrifying of all...

Almost all legends are said to be based on a true event. However, when stories are retold again and again, it is common for each narrator to add a little in and leave a little out, and so the story changes over time. The legend of the *Flying Dutchman* is said to have originated from an actual boat that sank in the waters off the Cape of Good Hope, South Africa, in the 17th century.

One day, so the story goes, Captain Hendrick van der Decken, otherwise known as "the Dutchman," set sail on his ship, the *Flying Dutchman.* At first, the ship flew across the sea as it headed for the captain's home in Amsterdam, in the Netherlands. Then, a fierce storm began to swirl around the boat, tossing it back and forth from colossal wave to colossal wave. The crew begged and pleaded with their captain to turn around and save them all. But the Dutchman refused and sailed on, farther and farther into the ferocious storm. Then all at once, a thunderous crack ripped through the sky as the hull was torn in two. Defiant to the end, the Dutchman cried out, "I will not die—I will sail on until the end of time," as his crew drowned in the lashing waves.

And so it is said that the *Flying Dutchman* is cursed to sail the seven seas for eternity, bringing bad luck to anyone who lays eyes on it.

One explanation for the eerie sightings of the *Flying Dutchman* is a type of mirage called Fata Morgana. This is when, by a trick of the light, a ship on the far horizon appears to be floating well above the water.

Troubled waters

For as long as boats have sailed the seas, sailors have told stories of ghostly galleons and phantom ships.

Lady Lovibond

Accounts of the sightings of the phantom *Lady Lovibond* told of the sound of party music coming from the ship.

Just off the Kent coast in southeast England lies the Goodwin Sands. This treacherous sandbank is 10 miles (14 km) long and appears above the waves at low tide before disappearing again at high tide. Since the first recorded shipwreck in 1298, over 2,000 ships have been wrecked here.

One legend tells of the *Lady Lovibond*, which set sail from England in 1748 to celebrate the captain's marriage. It was decked out with party lights, and a band was playing. The crew was in a lively mood—all except one. The ship's first mate, second in command to the captain, was in the unfortunate position of being in love with the captain's new wife. In a fit of jealousy, as the captain danced with his bride, the first mate steered the *Lady Lovibond* straight toward the Goodwin Sands. The boat sank, taking everyone on board down with her.

It is said that every fifty years since that tragic day, a ghostly *Lady Lovibond* can be seen sailing close to the Goodwin Sands.

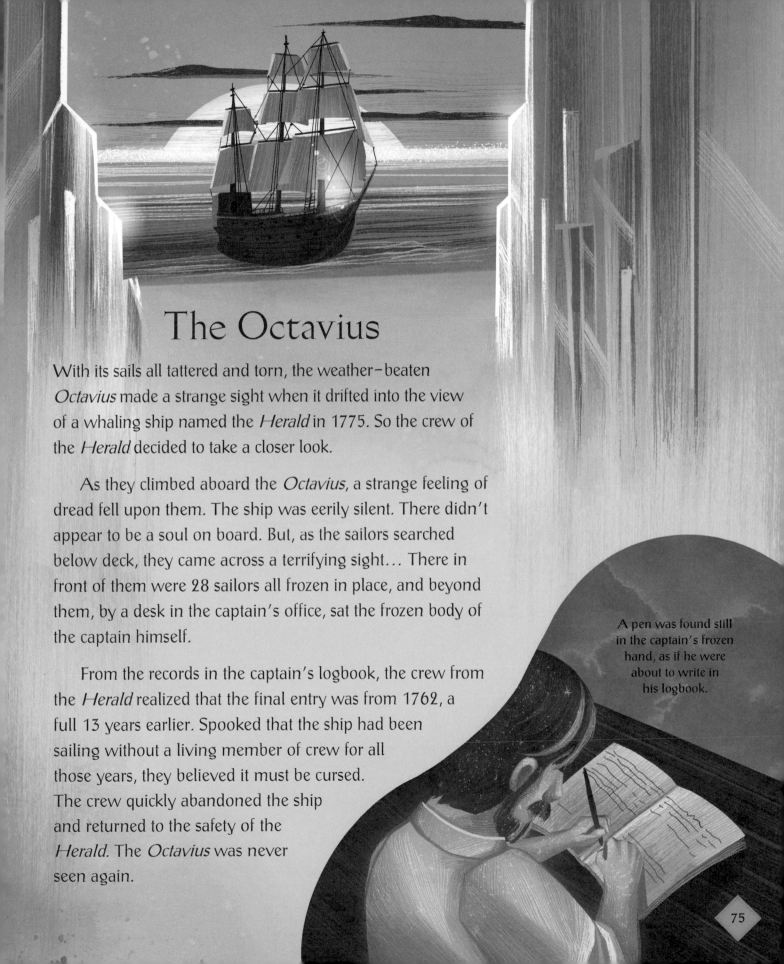

The Octavius

With its sails all tattered and torn, the weather-beaten *Octavius* made a strange sight when it drifted into the view of a whaling ship named the *Herald* in 1775. So the crew of the *Herald* decided to take a closer look.

As they climbed aboard the *Octavius*, a strange feeling of dread fell upon them. The ship was eerily silent. There didn't appear to be a soul on board. But, as the sailors searched below deck, they came across a terrifying sight… There in front of them were 28 sailors all frozen in place, and beyond them, by a desk in the captain's office, sat the frozen body of the captain himself.

From the records in the captain's logbook, the crew from the *Herald* realized that the final entry was from 1762, a full 13 years earlier. Spooked that the ship had been sailing without a living member of crew for all those years, they believed it must be cursed. The crew quickly abandoned the ship and returned to the safety of the *Herald.* The *Octavius* was never seen again.

A pen was found still in the captain's frozen hand, as if he were about to write in his logbook.

Amelia Earhart took off to fly around the world and was never seen again.

Amelia Earhart

The pioneering American aviator who mysteriously disappeared...

Amelia Mary Earhart was born on July 24, 1897, in Kansas, and from the start she had a strong sense of adventure. After seeing an airshow in Toronto, Canada, she made up her mind then that she wanted to fly. Not long after she bought her own aircraft. Amelia Earhart went on to break several aviation records. In 1932, she was the first woman to fly solo across the Atlantic Ocean, and she became a role model for women everywhere.

On June 1, 1937, Amelia Earhart and her aircraft navigator, Fred Noonan, left Miami, Florida, and attempted to fly around the world. Their trip was carefully planned and divided up into smaller flights to allow for refueling. On July 2, they took off in search of Howland Island—an uninhabited coral island in the

In a letter to her husband, Earhart wrote, "Women must try to do things as men have tried. When they fail, their failure must be but a challenge to others."

Pacific Ocean. It was on this journey that Amelia Earhart, her navigator, and her plane completely and mysteriously disappeared. An extensive mission was sent out—one of the biggest air and sea searches in American history—and more than 60 aircraft and several ships scoured the ocean.

Finally, the search was called off and Amelia Earhart was officially declared dead on January 5, 1939. However, people did not stop wondering what had happened to the famous aviator.

Amelia Earhart was never found. To this day, no one has been able to explain what happened or how she completely disappeared. Over the years, there have been many theories about her fate. One was that she returned to the USA and assumed another identity, another was that she became a castaway on a desert island. However, it appears most likely that Amelia Earhart's plane ran out of fuel and crashed into the Pacific Ocean.

Amelia's route to circumnavigate the globe would have involved flying 27,000 miles (43,450 km).

Hauntings

From ghostly underground bagpipers to skeletons trapped in walls, the world's most haunted places are overflowing with strange, supernatural happenings.

Dragsholm Slot

Built in 1215, Dragsholm Slot is one of the oldest castles in Denmark. With over 100 ghosts floating around its turrets, it is probably also the most haunted! One such ghost is the White Lady, who is said to wander the halls in her nightgown.

Château de Brissac

This imposing château, built originally in the 11th century and considered the tallest in France, is host to the ghost of the Green Lady (La Dame Verte). Standing in the chapel room wearing a long green dress, it is said that her sad moans can be heard throughout the castle.

Edinburgh Castle

Over 200 years ago, a network of tunnels was discovered beneath Edinburgh Castle in Scotland. A lone piper was sent in to explore. He played his bagpipes as he walked beneath the ground, but then the sound stopped and he was never seen again. On quiet days, the faint sound of bagpipes still haunts the castle above.

Banff Springs Hotel

One of Canada's spookiest buildings, first opened in 1888, is haunted by a collection of ghostly past guests. A bride is frequently spotted dancing in the hotel's ballroom in her bridal gown. Then there is the specter of a former bellhop, who helps guests to their rooms before disappearing into thin air.

St. Augustine lighthouse

Over the last 100 years, many lives have
been lost in or around the grounds of the
old St. Augustine lighthouse in Florida.
Some people believe that those who died
never really left. One lingering ghost is
said to belong to a lighthouse keeper, and
that his cigar smoke still fills the air.

Hoia-Baciu Forest

Paranormal activity is regularly
reported in this Transylvanian
forest in Romania. Most eerie
events occur in a clearing where no
plants or trees grow, and scientists are
unable to explain why. There have been
many disappearances since around the
1960s—the strangest involved a shepherd
and his flock of sheep.

Underwater graveyard

In 1944, a major World War II battle was
fought over the Chuuk Islands of Micronesia.
Over 4,500 soldiers lost their lives. Warships
and aircraft were destroyed in the battle and
sank to the bottom of the sea. This wreckage
has become the largest underwater graveyard
in the world, haunted by the ghosts of the
soldiers who tragically died.

La Recoleta Cemetery

The opulent Recoleta Cemetery in Buenos Aires, Argentina, is the final resting place of many important people, including politician and activist Eva Perón and many former presidents of Argentina. It is said that you can hear the ghostly caretaker's keys jangling as he tends to the graves.

Al Madam

An abandoned ghost town called Al Madam lies outside Sharjah, in the United Arab Emirates. Built around 1970–80, the houses are now filling up with sand, and no one is really sure why the town was deserted. Local rumors tell of a mysterious creature called a jinn causing havoc among the residents.

Xunantunich

This ancient site of the Maya civilization is in Belize in Central America. Local legend tells of the ruins being haunted by the Stone Woman. It is said that she appears in front of the ruin, climbs the stone stairs, and then disappears inside. She is dressed entirely in white with eyes as red as fire embers.

Winchester Mystery House

This 19th century mansion house in California is known for its ghostly apparitions, and people come from all over to visit the house. Both staff and guests have made reports of unexplained sightings. One active spirit is said to be the ghost of a gardener who once worked there.

Poveglia island

This small island in Venice, Italy, became the burial ground for the victims of the Plague—a pandemic in the 1340s. Sadly, many people died. To avoid further spread of the disease, the bodies were taken by boat to Poveglia. Ever since, locals have reported hearing cries and seeing ghostly figures wandering the island.

Himeji Castle

For over 400 years, tales of curious happenings have crept out of this magnificent fortress in Japan. One story concerns the ghost of a young maid accused of a crime she didn't commit. She is said to have been thrown into a well in the castle grounds and was seen counting out plates before disappearing.

83

The Curse of Kariba Dam

*When work began on the Kariba Dam,
the peaceful lives of the BaTonga people were shattered...*

The Zambezi valley in east Africa was home to the BaTonga people, who lived there peacefully for centuries. Their houses were built along the banks of the Zambezi River, which provided them with plentiful fresh water and fish. They lived in harmony with the natural world around them.

When construction of the colossal Kariba Dam began in the 1950s, the plans included flooding a large area of the Zambezi valley, forcing the BaTonga people out of their homes. The people were hopeful that their god Nyaminyami would stop the construction and help them return to their land, so they moved higher up the valley to wait for their god to act.

Just as the dam was about to be finished, a huge storm struck the area and filled the great river until it burst its banks and destroyed much of the dam. After this disaster, experts came to the conclusion that another storm that huge was unlikely to happen again soon. However, the following rainy season, a massive storm struck yet again, destroying newly built parts of the dam. It was almost as though a curse had been cast on the dam...

The Zambezi river god Nyaminyami is described as having the body of a snake and the head of a fish, and it is said that he stained the river water red as he swam through it. The BaTonga people believed that the new dam separated the river god from his wife.

Animal ghosts

Sightings of animal ghosts have happened throughout history. Often, these animal spirits return to a site—either to guard their beloved owners or for less well-meaning reasons. Who knows, perhaps these ghostly creatures may live on after death, leaping between this world and the spirit realm.

The Tower of London bear

There is said to be a ghostly bear who haunts the Tower of London in England. Stories date from the 1800s, and the phantom bear is so terrifying that it's claimed that anyone who lays eyes on it will die.

Greyfriars Bobby

John Gray and his pet dog, Bobby, walked the streets of Edinburgh in Scotland for years until John died in 1858 and was buried at Greyfriars cemetery. It is said that Bobby stayed by his master's grave for 14 years until his own death, and his spirit is said to sit there still.

The dragon pillar on Yan'an Gaojia

At first, builders could not seem to drill at the Yan'an Gaojia road in Shanghai, China. Then, after taking a monk's advice, they honored a dragon that was said to live on the site. The building work could then begin, and the finished road features a pillar decorated with dragons.

A glowing lion

One day in the 1930s, a zookeeper was out walking in a park near London Zoo, England, when he saw a glowing lion. The zookeeper recognized the lion and felt it could mean the animal was ill. On returning to work the next day, he was told that a lion had died the previous evening.

The Blue Dog

For over 200 years, in the town of Port Tobacco, Maryland, it is said that the Blue Dog, a large bluetick hound, stands guard over his master's buried treasure. Apparently, the dog howls at the site and charges at any treasure hunters if they dare come near.

The Demon Cat

In 1898, eight perfect paw prints mysteriously appeared in the floor of The United States Capitol Building in Washington, DC. It seemed to confirm rumors of a "Demon Cat" stalking the corridors, casting curses on anyone who saw it.

A vengeful horse

A horse that was killed in battle at the site of Akershus Castle, in Oslo, Norway, is believed to haunt the grounds. The horse is said to rear up and gallop straight at visitors before disappearing without trace.

CHAPTER 5

FASCINATING PHENOMENA

Nature has a magic all of its own,
capable of producing spectacular
light shows, rainbow mountains,
multicolored pools, and
never-ending lightning storms.
As an audience, we humans can only
look on in amazement at wonders that
dance far beyond our imaginations.

On the coast of Northern Ireland lies an extraordinary sight. Thousands of stone pillars create a staircase leading into the sea. These steps are known as the Giant's Causeway.

Battle of the giants

The legend of the Giant's Causeway

Looming large, one over the coast of Ireland and one over the coast of Scotland, were two giants—Finn McCool, in Ireland, and Benandonner the Red, in Scotland. Along with other kinds of giant activities such as stomping and pulling up trees with their bare hands, the two giants spent A LOT of time shouting at each other across the North Sea. Insults and threats hurtled back and forth like weapons over the waves, faster than eagles and angrier than (some) dragons.

Benandonner's name means "house of thunder." Finn McCool's name in Gaelic is Fionn Mac Cumhaill.

One day, McCool became so furious with Benandonner that he decided to challenge him to a battle. But first, McCool had to get across to Scotland. So, after a great deal of thinking and a particularly good wild boar sandwich, the giant picked up some massive rocks and started to carve them into stepping stones, until finally he had thousands of them. He built a bridge across the sea and strode over to Scotland. On reaching its shores, McCool snuck up on a snoring Benandonner...

In one long glance from his hairy toes up to the tip of his humungous ears, McCool saw that Benandonner the Red was far, far, bigger up close than he had looked from way across the sea on the Irish shore. Without stopping to take another look, McCool spun around and fled as fast as he could back to Ireland. But Benandonner heard McCool as he thundered back across the bridge, and he rose up and followed him home.

91

In a panic, McCool ran straight to his wife, Oonagh, and told her what had happened. Thinking quickly, the clever Oonagh grabbed a sheet and wrapped her husband up in it like a baby. As soon as she finished tucking him in, she ran around making more preparations.

A thunderous knock landed on their front door. After opening it, Oonagh looked up and up at Benandonner. She apologized that her husband was not there because he had gone off across Ireland to hunt for a herd of deer for their supper. Oonagh then politely offered him a homemade snack after his long journey and served him bread, baked with an iron rod inside. "This is McCool's favorite bread," she said as she handed it over. Benandoner took one bite and broke all of his front teeth.

Next, Oonagh showed him around their house, pointing out weapons so colossal that McCool himself could never have lifted them. This included a tree, which Oonagh said was one of McCool's spears. (When getting ready for his arrival, she had prepared a fallen tree, tying on a sharp head made from a shovel). The giant began to tremble slightly at the size of it.

Finally, she took him to meet their "baby." Benandonner took one glance at this truly gigantic child wrapped up in a sheet and imagined just how big the father must be—a giant so large that it used trees for spears and ate iron bars for snacks. Quickly deciding that there was no way that he could fight a giant of such a size, and scared that McCool would return and find him there, he fled out of the door and back across the giant stone steps, running with such force that he destroyed nearly all of them as he went.

Almost as extraordinary as the legendary Tale of the Giants is the science behind the formation of the Giant's Causeway rocks.

The Giant's Causeway is a stretch of over 40,000 mostly hexagonal, column-like rocks of varying heights. Although most of these rocky columns have five sides, some have been found with up to eight sides. The tallest column is around 39 ft (12 m) high—that is around the same height as a three-story house!

How did it form?

So how did it form! Around 50 million years ago, volcanic activity forced burning-hot lava up through the chalk beds that form the land there, before it cascaded back down into the bitterly cold sea. Where the hot lava met the cold sea, it cooled and contracted, causing these unusual columns of volcanic rock to form.

Hot lava was pushed up through gaps in the Earth's crust...

The lava cooled and contracted...

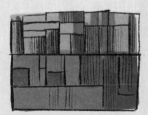
and created hexagonal-shaped columns.

Rainbows

They appear, miraculously, out of thin air, a magnificent, magical event to behold as they light up the skies... We look at rainbows with the same wonder that millions of people across the world and throughout history have done. Like the sun, the moon, and the stars, rainbows unify humans and inspire myths and legends. From the Rainbow Serpent of Aboriginal legend, to the gods of Japan who slid down a rainbow from heaven one day, almost every culture has a story about rainbows.

North America

In one Native American Cherokee myth, the rainbow is said to be the edge of the sun's coat, swirling beautifully around the Earth.

Japan

A Japanese legend tells of Izanami-no-miko and Izanagi-no-mikoto, a wife and husband, who hold between them a sacred, jeweled spear. Descending along a floating rainbow bridge to Earth, they stir up the ocean of chaos. From the ocean drops, falling from the tip of the spear, Japan is formed.

Australia

Across Australia, the myths and legends of the Aboriginal Rainbow Serpent tell of the Earth's creation by an extraordinary creature that took the form of a rainbow as it moved between water, land, and air.

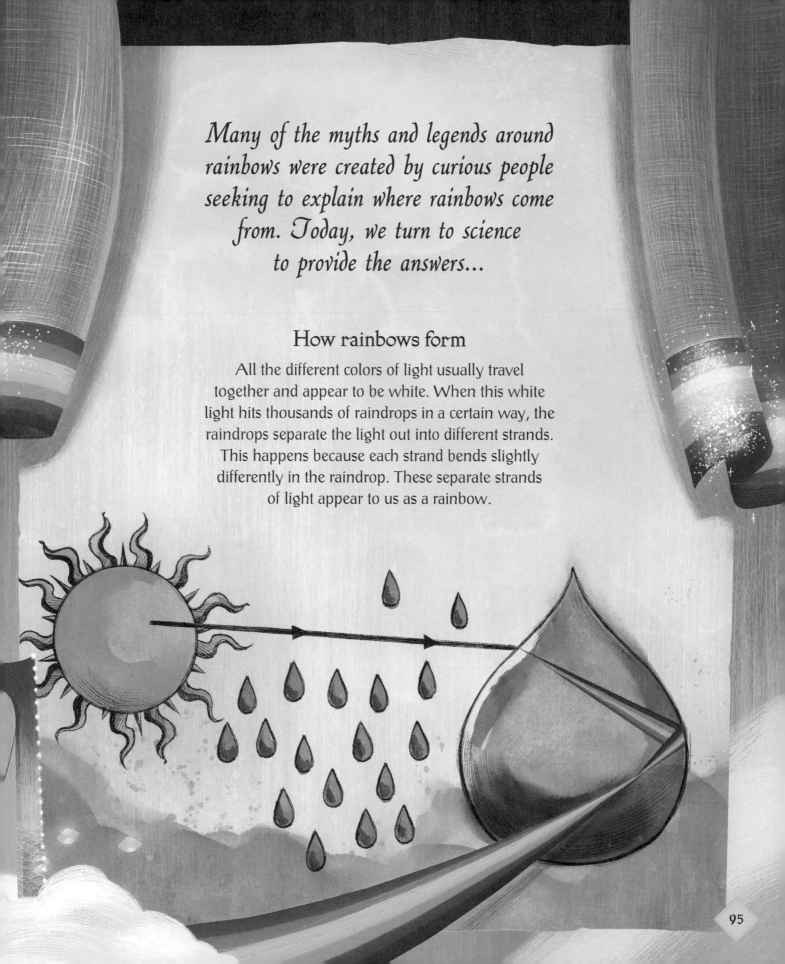

Many of the myths and legends around rainbows were created by curious people seeking to explain where rainbows come from. Today, we turn to science to provide the answers...

How rainbows form

All the different colors of light usually travel together and appear to be white. When this white light hits thousands of raindrops in a certain way, the raindrops separate the light out into different strands. This happens because each strand bends slightly differently in the raindrop. These separate strands of light appear to us as a rainbow.

Natural phenomena

Nature is the greatest magician of them all,
conjuring up majestic marvels beyond the
wildest wonders of our imaginations...

Rainbow Mountains

So extraordinary are the Rainbow Mountains in
northwest China, that if you came across them by
accident, you might think that you had fallen into
a fairy tale. The colorful stripes are caused by the
build up of different-colored minerals over millions
of years, which are then brightened by exposure
to oxygen in the air. These striped mountains
look almost magical in the way they light
up the landscape!

Spotted Lake

The aptly named Spotted Lake is a salty lake in the eastern Similkameen Valley of British Columbia, Canada. It is a sacred lake of the Syilx People of the Okanagan Nation, and the water is thought to have great healing properties. Rich minerals that have washed down from the surrounding hills collect in the water in high concentrations, creating the spots of many different colors.

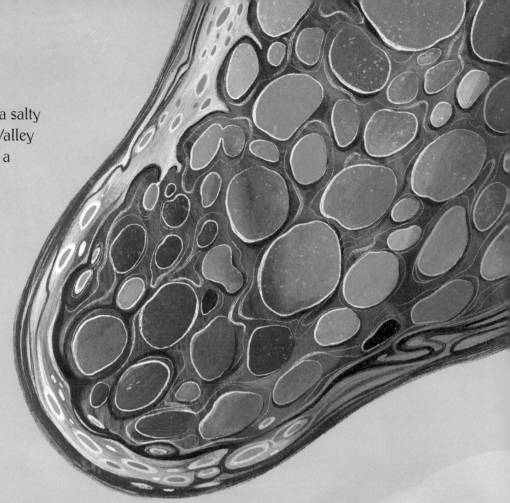

The Gates of Hell

The Darvaza gas crater in Turkmenistan is also known as the "Gates of Hell." This crater is a burning pit of natural gases, which were set on fire following a mining accident in the 1970s. The site was being drilled when an underground cavern collapsed into a deep crater, spewing out toxic gases like a giant cauldron. The gases were set on fire to prevent them from spreading, and they are still burning today.

Blood rain

Cases of blood rain have been recorded since ancient times, and until about 400 years ago, the rain was believed to be real blood and to be a sign of bad luck. The red color of the rain seems to happen when large concentrations of red dust particles become mixed in with the rainwater.

Blood Falls

Located in Antarctica, the Blood Falls on the tongue of a glacier confused scientists for many years. However, in 2017, imaging under the glacier revealed why the waterfalls are red and flow instead of freeze. The new imaging uncovered a subglacial river and lake, high in iron, giving the Falls its red color and brine, which helps to prevent it from freezing.

Rainbow eucalyptus

Found in the tropical rainforests of Indonesia, Papua New Guinea, and the Philippines, the colorful trunks of these beautiful trees occur because of the way that they shed thin layers of bark. Over time, as the green inner layer is exposed to the air, it ages at different times, creating a multitude of shades—reds, blues, purples, pinks, and oranges—all in a patchwork rainbow.

Fire whirls

These devastating natural phenomena can occur anywere in the world when hot winds come into contact with blazing bushfires. The combination can create a whirling column of fire that swirls in an upward direction, sweeping up ash and debris, and reaching temperatures of over 1,832°F (1,000°C) at their core.

Light phenomena

Even everyday beams of sunlight that dapple the ground as they fall through the leaves of trees can feel magical, and nature has produced many more phenomenal light shows.

Light shows

Rivers of light dance across the sky at the poles of our planet. At the North Pole they are called the aurora borealis, or northern lights, while at the South Pole they are called the aurora australis, or southern lights.

The lights occur when a solar wind hits the Earth from the sun. The particles create different-colored light as they reach the atmosphere. Earth's magnetic field pulls the particles toward the poles, causing flowing patterns in the sky.

Bioluminescent bay

This underwater light display happens in bays in just a few parts of the world, including the Caribbean island of Puerto Rico. The lights are a rare but stunning sight—so bright that water is illuminated at night in a gentle glow.

The blue-green neon glow is caused by organisms called dinoflagellates, which produce their own light. The narrow openings of certain bays and lagoons cause the organisms to cluster together.

Naga fireballs

Along the Mekong River in Asia, different-sized balls of red light rise up before exploding into nothing. Known as Naga fireballs, local legend tells of a great river serpent, named Naga, who breathes balls of fire.

Mystery surrounds this phenomenon, although some scientific explanations have been put forward. A natural build up of riverbed gases may be the cause, or perhaps the firing of flares—but nobody really knows.

Never-ending storm

Appearing almost every night and lasting up to 10 hours at a time, the Catatumbo lightning storm in Venezuela sees an average of 28 bolts of lightning per minute strike the ground on more than 300 nights of the year.

The "never-ending storm" is found at the point where the Catatumbo River flows into a lake. Cool air from the mountains and warm air from the Caribbean meet here, creating the perfect conditions for fierce storms of lightning.

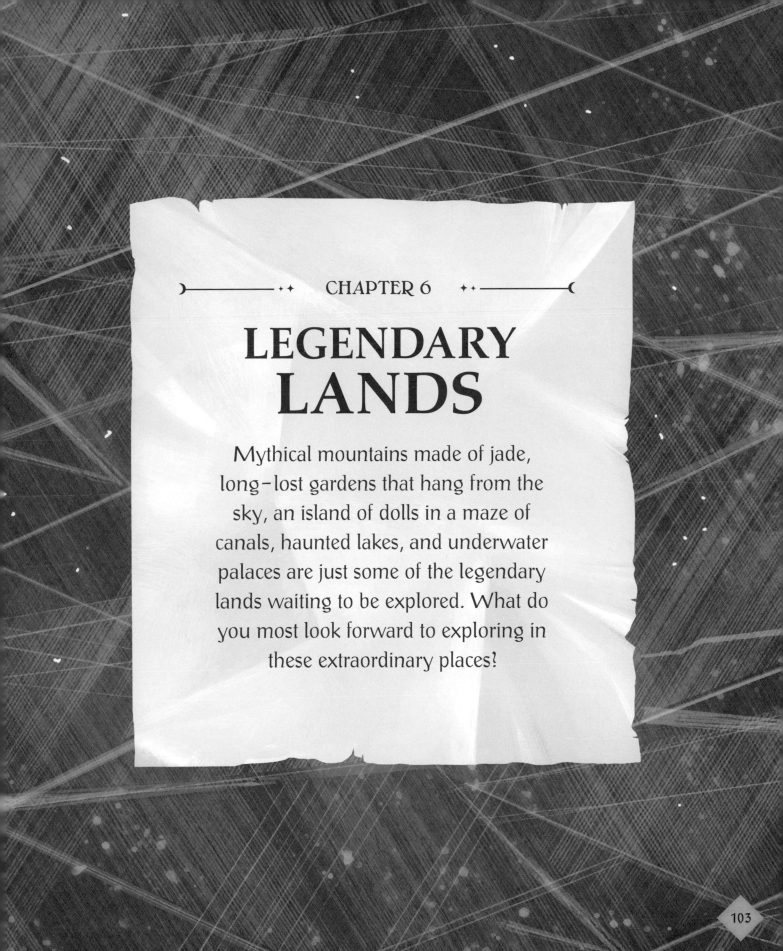

CHAPTER 6

LEGENDARY LANDS

Mythical mountains made of jade, long-lost gardens that hang from the sky, an island of dolls in a maze of canals, haunted lakes, and underwater palaces are just some of the legendary lands waiting to be explored. What do you most look forward to exploring in these extraordinary places!

Jade Mountain

*A mythical, bejeweled mountain,
home to an ancient Chinese goddess*

The crane is just one of the
many types of birds that are
said to make their home
on the legendary
Jade Mountain.

The Kunlun Mountains
are a real-life range of
mountains steeped in myth.

Sweeping across central China like a dragon's tail, the Kunlun Mountains divide the north of the country from the south. This range is so old that it is known as the Ancestor of Ten Thousand Mountains. And some people say that in among these ancient hills that loom high into the sky, there stands the legendary Jade Mountain.

For centuries, Jade Mountain was revered as a sacred site for Taoism—an ancient Chinese philosophy. Central to Taoist beliefs is an understanding that humans and all other animals should live in balance and harmony with the universe (Tao), and that the spirit of the body is immortal and rejoins the universe after death.

Jade Mountain is surrounded by jeweled gardens full of peach trees and multicolored, magical fungi. Here lives Xi Wangmu, one of the oldest goddesses in China. Her name is usually translated as "Queen Mother of the West." This goddess's powers are wide-ranging and far-reaching, from controlling the cosmic forces of time and space to determining the life-spans of all living beings. And her majestical home on Jade Mountain is believed to be the portal between heaven and Earth.

Wonders of Jade Mountain

Throughout history and across continents, humans have searched for a legendary place that is free from all suffering—a place where wisdom, kindness, and laughter help humans to live in harmony with nature and one another. Jade Mountain is said to be such a place. Here are just some of the enchanting features that are said to be found there.

Jewel-like rocks

The rocks of Jade Mountain are said to contain precious stones. When the rocks are broken open, their bright insides lie glittering in piles around the beautiful gardens that surround the mountain.

Birds and animals

An array of creatures, both real and mythical, make their home on the mythical mountain. Cranes, tigers, and yaks strut alongside mythical beings, and all live in harmony together.

Immortal humans

The eight immortal humans in Chinese mythology represent male, female, the old, the young, the rich, the poor, the noble, and the humble. These celestial beings are said to feast on top of Jade Mountain.

Feast

A "Feast of Peaches" is said to be held on the third day of the third month. During this feast, the ripe peaches of immortality would be served to the immortal humans at a grand banquet.

Towering cliffs

Sometimes, Jade Mountain is described as a pillar from Earth to heaven, with towering cliffs of glimmering jade. The mountain is said to reach as far down into the Earth as it does up to the sky.

Exotic jeweled plants

Among the gardens of Jade Mountain, you'll find enchanted orchards. Here, pearls and rare jewels grow on trees, ready to be picked and woven into beautiful pieces of jewelry.

Magical fungi

Blooming into extraordinary forms, painted in majestic colors, and brimming with magical powers, special fungi grow beneath the jeweled plants that grow in the gardens.

The Goddess Xiwangmu

The Goddess Xiwangmu, or Queen Mother of the West, is a mountain spirit transformed into human form. It is said of her that "nobody knows her beginning, and no one knows her end."

Peaches

In the middle of Xiwangmu's garden, said to be the very center of the universe, grows a giant peach tree. The peaches appear only every few thousand years, and they grant eternal life to those who eat them.

Azure birds

The Goddess Xiwangmu is said to be looked after by the azure birds, who bring her berries and other food. These mythical birds circle Jade Mountain and keep guard.

Island of the Dolls

A strange and haunting tale of how a small island came to be overgrown with trees full of dolls...

There lies a canal system in a district of Mexico City, in Mexico, called Xochimilco, which dates back to the time of the Aztecs. In the midst of this maze of canals and lakes is a chinampa, or small island, called the Isla de las Munecas—the Island of the Dolls.

The story goes that one sad morning, the island's caretaker came across a girl who had fallen into the canal and tragically drowned. There was nothing he could do to save her, and he was devestated by her death. Then a few days later, he saw a doll that he assumed to have been the girl's floating on the canal. The caretaker placed the doll in one of the trees on the island so that the girl's spirit could find it again.

Xochimilco is best known for its maze of canals built at the time of the Aztec empire (1300–1521).

The caretaker had been very shaken by his experience of finding the poor girl, and the memory haunted him. Each night, he thought he could hear the girl whispering and the sound of her footsteps. He wanted to make the girl's spirit happy so that she could rest in peace. And so he collected more and more dolls and placed them in the trees around the island for the spirit to play with.

Today, local people and tourists travel over to the island on brightly colored boats, called *trajineras*, bringing even more dolls to keep the spirit of the girl happy.

Scholomance

Have you ever found yourself daydreaming in your classroom and imagined the other kinds of schools you could be attending instead?

You may have dreamed about learning to balance at the very top of the tent at a circus academy or becoming chief cake-taster at an amazing baking school. Or, perhaps you could even imagine mastering the dark arts of magical powers, at a school named Scholomance, where the headmaster's nickname is "Mr. Devil!"

Romanian folklore tells of just such a subterranean school of dark magic found deep underground. This is a very selective school, with only around 11 students. Once enrolled, pupils follow a strict timetable of strange lessons, and they are not allowed to go above ground or see sunlight for seven years. No one is entirely sure who the principal really is, or what becomes of the pupils at the end of their training…

On concluding their studies, the top student is chosen as the Weathermaker. They are given a dragon to ride around the world to control the weather. The dragon lives deep down in a lake, in the mountains above Sibiu.

The entrance is a carefully guarded secret, hidden in a meandering maze of underground tunnels. But, if you are determined to keep looking, legend says that Scholomance is deep, deep down under the Transylvanian Alps, close to a place named Sibiu.

Once the capital of Transylvania, Sibiu is a beautiful Romanian city known as "The City with Eyes" because the houses there have two eyelike windows set high up in their rooftops. As the Scholomance students learn magic powers deep underneath the city, perhaps the people living there like to keep a constant lookout from up high...

Studying at Scholomance

The students at Scholomance are expected to study hard during their seven years underground. To create suitable study conditions, the teachers—who are senior spell-casters—use their magic to grow gardens, forests, and jungles in the subterranean mountain caves. At the end of the seven years, there is a final exam. Scholomance pupils are required to write out everything that they have learned in the Scholomance *Book of Knowledge.*

Weather

One of the main aims of Scholomance is to find the next Weathermaker, so weather-conjuring lessons are crucial. They include writing spells for brewing up thunder in steaming mountaintop lakes, charging up thunderbolts, and stirring up tornadoes.

Casting spells

The weather spells often need to be cast in midair while riding on the back of the school dragon. This takes a high level of skill and a great deal of practice. To create the ideal conditions below ground, teachers create storm tunnels for students to fly through.

Dragon training

Although only the top student is presented with a unique weather dragon, all the students need to learn dragon training. Upon arrival at Scholomance, they are each given their own baby dragon to train. At the end of the seven years, their dragons will be fully grown.

Nature

Nature holds great powers, and all of the ingredients for Scholomance spells are gathered from it. The students are taught how to harness the most-prized ingredients, including colors sucked from rainbows, sap from maple trees, and venom from snakes and toads.

Languages

Learning the languages of every plant and creature is essential. Each day, a lesson focuses on a different species. Some are more difficult to learn than others. Birdsong tends to be quick and easy to pick up, while cactus-speak usually takes much longer to master.

Dragon care

Raising a dragon from a baby requires a great deal of patience. Among many other skills, pupils need to know how to help their young dragons control their fire breathing. Accidental bonfires in dormitories are a frequent occurrence.

Chanting

Casting spells requires skilled chanting. Being out of tune or forgetting the words might give incorrect results. This could have dangerous consequences—it might for instance turn a fellow student into a vampire instead of a hungry vampire into a vegetarian!

Silent Spell Study

There are often actions to learn, as well as words, when studying spells. During Silent Spell Study, students concentrate on memorizing actions such as waving their arms over cauldrons, sweeping their long cloaks in arcs, and sprinkling powdered potions around in silence.

Dragon riding

In the first few years, while their own dragons are too small to ride, pupils take turns practicing on the school dragon. Basic lessons include summoning the dragon out from its lair, steadying it at the mounting block, and making sure not to fall during takeoff and landing.

The Seven Wonders of the Ancient World

The Seven Wonders of the Ancient World were a list of magnificent human-made structures built by ancient civilizations in areas we today know as Greece, Turkey, Egypt, and Iraq. The buildings were so extraordinary they almost had to be seen to be believed.

The Lighthouse of Alexandria

This early lighthouse was built in the city of Alexandria, in Egypt. Construction began in 290 BCE, and it took almost 20 years to complete it. The lighthouse used mirrors to reflect light out to sea to warn sailors.

The Statue of Zeus

The ancient Greek sculptor Phidias created this huge statue of Zeus—the king of the gods—from ivory and gold. It stood in a temple in Olympia, in Greece. Zeus was shown sitting on a bejeweled wooden throne, holding a statue of Nike, the Greek goddess of victory.

The Great Pyramid of Giza

Completed in around 2560 BCE, the Great Pyramid of Giza, Egypt, is 449 ft (137 m) high, and it was the tallest building in the world for over 4,000 years. Along with two smaller pyramids, it was built as the final resting place of three Egyptian pharaohs. It is the only one of the Seven Wonders that is still standing.

The Temple of Artemis

This huge marble temple was built in honor of the Greek goddess Artemis. It was twice the size of any other Greek temple of the time, and it was said that the blocks of stone that sat above the many columns were so heavy that they could only have been lifted into place with the help of Artemis herself.

The Mausoleum of Halicarnassus

In around 353 BCE, the Mausoleum of Halicarnassus was built in present–day Turkey as a tomb for the Persian king Mausolus, to ensure that he would remain famous after his death. He employed only the finest sculptors, artists, and tradespeople to design and erect it.

The Hanging Gardens of Babylon

As well as being beautiful, the Hanging Gardens of Babylon, in present–day Iraq, were said to have used a highly advanced watering system that drew water up from ground level so that it cascaded down through garden terraces. This helped keep the plants watered in the desert heat.

The Colossus of Rhodes

This giant statue was built to honor the Greek sun god Helios in around 280 BCE. It stood in Mandraki Harbor, on the Greek island of Rhodes. Made of bronze, it was 98 ft (30 m) high. It was the tallest statue in the world but was destroyed by an earthquake in 226 BCE.

The Hanging Gardens of Babylon

A garden paradise that is one of the Seven Wonders of the Ancient World

Appearing to float like a cloud above a desert landscape, this garden of tiered terraces, beautiful plants, suspended walkways, and huge, brightly colored flower beds would have been an extraordinary sight in ancient times. So it is no surprise that such a place would become known as one of the Seven Wonders of the Ancient World.

What is perhaps a surprise though, is that there is doubt whether these magnificent gardens existed at all. According to legend, the Babylonian king Nebuchadnezzar II married Queen Amytis, who had journeyed to Babylon from her home in Media— a green and mountainous area. When she moved to hot, dry, Babylon, she missed her home. And so King Nebuchadnezzar built the beautiful Hanging Gardens to please her.

While Nebuchadnezzar II of Babylon (in present−day Iraq) was a real figure in history, the Hanging Gardens remain shrouded in mystery.

Detailed descriptions of the gardens left by ancient writers led to extensive archaeological searches to try to find them. However, today it remains the only one of the Seven Wonders of the Ancient World that has never been found. The most recent research suggests that they may not have been in Babylon at all, but in a place called Nineveh, which lies north of Babylon. The search continues…

Yggdrasil

In Norse myth, there is a tree called Yggdrasil that is so immense it holds within it nine whole worlds, brimming with gods, giants, and elves. A hideous dragon haunts its rotting roots, and its high leaves brush against the heavens. From its branches, the wondrous legends of Norse myth have been woven.

VANAHEIM

NIFLHEIM

JOTUNHEIM

Bifrost

Asgard and Midgard were linked together by Bifrost, a rainbow bridge that allowed the Aesir gods to visit Midgard. During the great battle of Ragnarok, the Frost and Fire Giants used the rainbow bridge to reach Asgard and slay the gods.

Vanaheim

A riot of forests, mountains, streams, and meadows overflow from the edges of this realm. The wise old gods of nature stroll through their land, meeting among the mounds and lakes to discuss the future.

Niflheim

Cloaked in a frosty mist and deep layers of ice, the rivers of Niflheim flow out beneath its frozen crust, carrying water to the other worlds.

Jotunheim

The Frost Giants, enemies of the Aesir gods, storm the icy mountains of Jotunheim, fighting their way through freezing winds, on to their next battle.

Asgard

The grandest of all the worlds,
Asgard is home to the Aesir, the top
tier of Nordic gods. Valhalla—the
Hall of the Slain—is found here.
It houses the souls of those who
fought bravely in battle, and its roof
is made from armored shields.

Alfheim

Given as a gift to the god Freyr,
this glorious realm of light and dark
is inhabited by elves—supernatural
beings said to be as bright and
radiant as the sun itself.

Muspelheim

This realm is a glowing furnace
that houses the Fire Giants, who
are enemies of the Aesir. The Fire
Giants' leader, Surtr, brandishes
a flaming sword as he stands
waiting for war.

Midgard

Encircled by a raging ocean in
which a fearsome sea serpent
swims, Midgard is the human
realm, similar to Earth. The Midgard
serpent is so enormous that it can
surround Midgard and still hold
its own tail in its mouth.

Helheim

This underworld realm
was the afterlife destination
for the dead who were not
heroic enough to enter Valhalla.

Svartalfheim

Working in a network
of subterranean mines and
forges deep underground are
the dwarves—the master
craftspeople of Norse legend.

ASGARD

BIFROST

ALFHEIM

MUSPELHEIM

MIDGARD

SVARTALFHEIM

HELHEIM

Ryūjin's Underwater Palace

If you should dive down to the bottom of the sea
off the coast of Japan, you might find a wondrous palace...

The trees in the gardens of this aquatic palace have emerald leaves and ruby berries, which skip and play in the watery currents.

Created from red and white coral, Rūyjin's Underwater Palace emerges from the seafloor as if it has grown from there, and spirals up, up though forty floors. This palace is the home of Ryūjin the dragon king, god of the sea, who is so powerful he can control the tides. In one claw, he grasps a bright blue gem to draw in the sea, and in the other, he grasps a white pearl to send the sea away again.

This palatial palace is divided into four separate areas, representing the four seasons—spring, summer, fall, and winter. Now, just imagine you are wandering through each section— what delights await you! Pink cherry blossoms will kiss your face in the spring tearooms. When you reach the summer pavilion, your ears will fill with the bright music of an orchestra of crickets. As you walk through the fall hall, brightly colored maple leaves in every shade of red, orange, and yellow will crunch under your feet. Then, as you enter the winter ballroom, you will see snowflakes dance in the icy light.

Be careful, though. Don't stay too long. According to legend, one hundred human years pass for each day spent in the palace...

CHAPTER 7

LOOKING FOR ALIEN LIFE

Do you ever gaze out on a starry night and wonder about the possibility of other life, staring back at us from beyond the darkness? If indeed there are other life-forms out there, where might they be, what could they look like, and will we ever meet them? And, if we do, will they be the aliens, or will we!

Flying saucers

When we think of a UFO, an image of a futuristic flying saucer carrying little green aliens might come floating across our minds. But are these ideas from fact or fiction?

Kenneth Arnold's distinctive description of the objects that he saw gave flying saucers their name.

Numerous books, TV programs, and films were inspired by the newspaper reports of the flying saucers. It filled people's imaginations with the possibilities of life on other planets.

On June 24, 1947, American aviator Kenneth Arnold was flying his private plane over Washington state when he saw an alarmingly bright flash ahead. It was followed by more flashes and then nine crescent-shaped objects appeared. They flew along in formation, dipping and rising together "like the tail of a kite." He later described the visibility that day as excellent and said that the objects "flew like a saucer if you skipped it across water."

At first, Kenneth Arnold had thought that he was seeing a flock of geese, or, as he got closer, some advanced military aircraft being tested. But the speed of the objects confused him. They were estimated to be traveling at around 1,660 mph (2,670 kph)—three times faster than any jet at the time.

Arnold reported his sighting, and it was picked up by many newspapers that ran headlines such as "Supersonic flying saucers sighted by Idaho pilot." The story sparked interest across the nation, and the term "flying saucers" became widely used in newspapers across the country.

Later, the term "unidentified flying objects" (UFOs) joined the now-popular phrase "flying saucers." In 2022, NASA (National Aeronautics and Space Administration) set up a scientific team to examine events in the sky that couldn't be explained by known aircraft or natural phenomena. The explanation for what Kenneth Arnold saw remains a mystery.

125

Playground UFO

Unexplained UFO sightings in a village in Wales...

When just one child claims to have seen a UFO, it might be easy to think that they could have been mistaken. However, when a whole class of children describes seeing the same UFO, all at the same time, it is perhaps not so easy to dismiss...

This is exactly what happened in the village of Broad Haven in Pembrokeshire, Wales. And it remains one of the most remarkable unexplained UFO sightings ever.

In 1977, a class of children from Broad Haven Primary School claimed they had seen a UFO landing in a field close to their playground. They described the craft as a silver object, shaped

There was a high number of other reported sightings in the area at around the same time. This phenomenon, in which multiple sightings are seen in one area, is known as a UFO flap.

like a torpedo with a curved dome on top of the middle section.

One child said that they didn't feel afraid when they saw it, but that they did feel a sense of "awe and wonderment."

The children's teachers didn't believe the children's reports, however. And so the pupils were separated from each other and asked to draw what they had seen. They all drew almost identical pictures of the craft.

Investigations into the sightings began, with a government department and local military police involved in trying to solve the mystery. People remained baffled, however. How was it possible that a whole class had lied! The mystery continues...

It is believed that practical jokers were behind some of the sightings. One local man came forward, years later, to say that he had dressed up in a silver suit in the area after hearing that a UFO had been spotted. But this still doesn't explain what the children saw...

UFO sightings

All of the UFO sightings below were caught by either ground sonar or radar, and were reported by reliable witnesses. They remain unexplained to this day.

Light cluster

When: Nighttime 1956

Where: Over the Atlantic Ocean

Witnesses: Commander George Benson and crew

Commander Benson of the US Marine Corps was flying with some 30 pilots, navigators, and flight engineers, using ground radar. As they flew, a cluster of lights were identified below their aircraft. One of these glowing objects broke away, tilted up, and flew alongside them before pulling ahead and flying off at an astonishing speed.

Hovering at the harbor

When: October 1967

Where: Shag Habour, Nova Scotia, Canada

Witnesses: Locals and military personnel

In Nova Scotia, Canada, a UFO with bright lights was spotted hovering above the water. It tilted at a right angle before dipping beneath the surface of the water and disappearing. A second one followed. They were spotted again days later, leaving the water.

Intense heat

When: November 1986

Where: Airspace above Anchorage, Alaska

Witnesses: Pilot Kenju Terauchi and crew

In the skies aboove Alaska, a UFO the size of an aircraft carrier flew in front of the Japan Airlines Boeing 747, Flight 1628. At one point, the UFO slowed down until it was so close that the pilot, Kenju Terauchi, could feel an intense heat coming from it before it disappeared.

Near-miss landing

When: April 1991

Where: Heathrow Airport, UK

Witnesses: Pilot Achille Zaghetti

While making a descent to land at Heathrow Airport, Italian pilot Achille Zaghetti reported to ground control that a cigar-shaped UFO had shot past his plane.

Ground control confirmed they had observed an unidentified object that had been following the plane for around 11 miles (18 km). The UK's Ministry of Defence could provide no explanation for the object.

129

UFO investigation

Top secret development and testing of spyware, surveillance equipment, and military aircraft may be responsible for a large number of reports of UFO sightings.

The Roswell Incident

UFO sightings had been big news in the summer of 1949 in the USA. It was during this summer that rancher W.W. Brazel and his son, Vernon, were driving across their land in New Mexico. With UFO reports fresh on his mind, it's not a surprise that when Brazel came across strange, shiny, wreckage scattered across his land, he immediately thought that it might have alien origins.

Once he had gathered up the pieces, he drove straight to a nearby airfield named Roswell. After inspecting the wreckage, the airbase issued a statement saying that they had recovered a crashed "flying disk."

The statement was quickly withdrawn, and a new one was put out to say that the wreckage was most likely from a weather balloon. But it was too late; many people were now suspicious that a real UFO event was being covered up.

Years later, in 1994, a report was published by the US Air Force that identified the crashed object as a nuclear test surveillance balloon.

Military aircraft

When new military aircraft are launched, they often look so different that it is entirely possible they could be mistaken for advanced alien spacecraft.

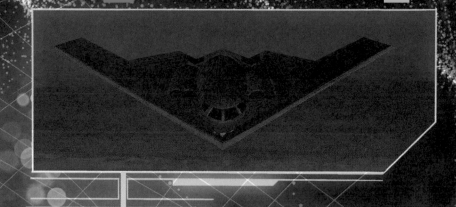

B-2 Spirit

Also known as the Stealth Bomber, this US aircraft remains one of the strangest-looking planes in the sky. With its groundbreaking batwing design, it looks as though it just swept out of an action film! Believing that it might have flown here from another world would be an easy mistake to make.

SR-71 Blackbird

This extraordinary surveillance plane was so fast that it could accelerate away from a missile to avoid being hit. Before drones were used for long-range aerial spying, the SR-71 Blackbird was the US military's secret weapon, and its sleek, black appearance gave it a truly futuristic look.

Eurofighter Typhoon

This European, multinational, delta-winged fighter plane was designed to be unstable in flight, allowing it to have exceptional maneuverability when taking part in airborne battles. It first took to the skies in 2008. Its extraordinary ability to swerve, dodge, climb, and dive was unlike anything that had come before.

UFO explanation...

So, could advanced military equipment account for all reported UFO sightings? While investigations of many UFOs have revealed them to be aircraft, balloons, clouds, or distant planets, a small percentage remains unidentified. We just have to accept that there are unsolved mysteries up there in our skies...

Area 51

*For many years, a strange place in the USA
known as Area 51 has been cloaked in mystery...*

High fences surround Area 51, a vast site located in a dry lake bed in Nevada. Armed guards patrol the perimeter, while electronic surveillance cameras follow every movement. Despite it being opened in 1955, the US government refused to acknowledge the existence of Area 51 until 2013. And, until recently, it did not appear on any maps.

This secret location, and the lack of information as to what it was, sparked the imagination of the nation, leading to wild claims and numerous conspiracy theories.

A number of people reported seeing UFOs in the area, while a few people even claimed that they had been abducted by aliens and then returned to Earth. An office was set up by the CIA (Central Intelligence Agency) just to deal with the number of UFO sightings being reported over Nevada.

The fences are covered in signs warning people to keep out. Taking photographs anywhere nearby is strictly forbidden.

Today, there is still very little official information available about Area 51. However, it is believed that the site was set up to develop and test spy planes, and now develops other advanced spyware. This would explain a lot of the secrecy as well as many of the UFO sightings— the new spy planes would have been a completely unfamiliar sight to anyone not used to seeing them.

With such a high level of mystery still surrounding the site, who knows what else could have happened there over the years...

Alien interaction

It is highly unlikely that any aliens we might meet would take a recognizable form. Just as we have evolved to live on Earth, any other life-forms out there will have developed to suit the environment on their own planet.

Will we know them when we see them?

Alien beings could be microscopic or colossal, a transparent gas or as solid as a rock. They might be so advanced that they take the form of something similar to artificial intelligence or move around unseen, perhaps as electrical pulses.

Aliens may even appear in completely different dimensions. As humans, we see in three dimensions: depth, length, and width. However, some alien forms may only appear in two dimensions. Imagine, for instance, an alien life-form that appears only as a shadow on a wall, or as a strange shape moving across a piece of paper.

Radio telescopes have been set up all around the world to listen out for any possible signals from alien life.

Have they already communicated with us?

Science has demonstrated such a strong case for the possible existence of life on other planets that we now have radio telescopes set up for listening out for any signals. The projects using these enormous radio telescopes are known as SETI: The Search for Extraterrestrial Intelligence.

In August 1977, American astronomer Jerry R. Ehman was studying the radio signals from Ohio State University's Big Ear radio telescope in the USA when he noticed a strange blip in the information. The signal that had appeared was incredibly strong but very brief. It lasted just one minute and twelve seconds.

Scientists from many fields have been unable to explain what caused the signal, and so its source remains a mystery. Could the explanation possibly be that it was a communication from another planet! We still don't know.

The astronomer was so amazed at what he had found that he wrote "Wow!" on the printout reading, which led to it being called the "Wow! signal."

Looking for life

All life on Earth needs water. So, when searching for alien life, scientists focus on places in our universe that may have water. While we don't know for sure where Earth's water came from, most scientists think that it arrived on one of the many asteroids that struck Earth billions of years ago. Liquid water requires certain conditions. When there is too much heat, water will evaporate; when it is too cold, water freezes. Here are some of the places in our solar system that scientists think could hold life—many, though not all, may once have held water.

Europa

A moon of Jupiter, Europa is one of the most promising contenders for holding alien life. Europa is covered in ice, and scientists think there could be a salty ocean lying underneath the ice where life could evolve.

Mars

The planet Mars was once covered with flowing water. Although this is no longer the case, Mars does share some characteristics with planet Earth. Scientists are investigating whether there are any signs of alien life in those areas of Mars that used to hold water.

The clouds of Venus

While the extreme temperatures on the surface of Venus make this planet an unlikely home for any living thing, the clouds in the atmosphere around Venus form a friendlier environment. Scientists think it's possible that incredibly tough organisms may exist there.

Ceres

Like many of the asteroids orbiting the sun in the asteroid belt, the dwarf planet Ceres holds a lot of water. In fact, after the Earth, it holds the second-largest amount of water in our solar system. This makes Ceres a logical place to explore for possible life.

Titan

Titan is Saturn's largest moon. Here, instead of water, methane rain falls, and the rivers, lakes, and seas are filled with liquid methane and ethane. Scientists studying this exceptional moon believe that these strange rivers, lakes, and seas may be habitable. The life that might form there, though, would be totally unlike anything on Earth.

Enceladus

The sixth-largest moon of Saturn, Enceladus is considered to be one of the strongest possibilities for alien life. Beneath its icy, reflective surface and erupting ice volcanoes lies an underground ocean. Scientists are investigating whether hydrothermal vents here could provide the right conditions for life.

Space hoppers

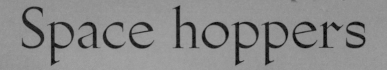

A theory called panspermia proposes that life, in the form of simple bacteria, could exist in the universe and might be able to travel between planets.

Hitchiking on astronauts

From 2009, the Japanese Aerospace Exploration Agency (JAXA) carried out experiments to investigate whether bacteria can survive in outer space. Cells of the bacteria *Deinococcus* were sent to the International Space Station (ISS)—an orbiting laboratory where scientists and astronauts live and work in space. When the samples were studied back on Earth, the scientists found that some of the bacteria had survived.

Research scientists involved in the study have said that if bacteria can survive in space, then bacteria may be transferred from one planet to another. It's not impossible that if life started on Mars, say, then that this could have been transferred to Earth. And it would follow from this that we are the offspring of Martian life.

Great lengths are taken to stop any harmful bacteria from hitchhiking on humans traveling out to the ISS. However, as humans are full of friendly bacteria, and shed hair and skin cells constantly, the chance that we have accidentally introduced bacteria into space is very high.

Hopping on an asteroid

In the early days of its existence, Earth was regularly hit by meteorites. And it was not just meteorites—an entire planet, named Theia, smashed into ours around 4.5 billion years ago.

Could some form of microscopic life have landed on Earth after hopping on a planet or asteroid? We know that bacteria are capable of surviving in the most extreme conditions, but space is vast and the journey would be long.

In 2020, Japanese scientists were able to revive bacteria that had been dormant at the bottom of the ocean for 100 million years. This could be one way for organisms to survive the journey—by falling asleep. But what about the impact on landing? Smashing into Earth on a meteorite would not be gentle. Could anything survive the collision?

There are still many more things about panspermia to be investigated, but even the possibility that we might have landed here from Mars is an amazing thought.

Bacteria have been shown to survive this level of impact as long as they are tucked deep inside of fractures in the rock.

CHAPTER 8

BIG QUESTIONS

From the gargantuan to the unimaginably small, there are many questions about our universe, but can science answer them all? Does it tell us what friendship looks like and how we can measure it? Does it explain why humans appear to want to destroy the Earth that feeds and protects them? And, if science doesn't have the answers, where do we look for them?

What made the universe?

Have you ever wondered how you came to be here? Could we all be avatars running around in a giant computer game, built by an advanced form of artificial intelligence? Or, did an almighty being create everything from nothing? These are just a couple of the many possibilities. However, you might also ask, what created the artificial intelligence or the almighty being?

Solid

Liquid

Matter

The theory is that space, time, and matter all began with the Big Bang. Starting tinier than an atom, the universe began to expand at a fantastic rate and then began to cool. As the temperature dropped, some of the energy from the explosion changed into matter in the form of solids, liquids, and gases.

The Big Bang

The most widely accepted theory for how the universe came to be is called the Big Bang theory. Most scientists agree that the universe was created in an explosion more than 13 billion years ago. But what created the Big Bang is an ongoing scientific mystery.

Galaxies appear

First stars appear

Dark Ages

Big Bang

Time

Gas

Plasma

Supernovas

Like the Big Bang,
a supernova is a massive
explosion, but it affects a single
star rather than the whole universe.
Sometimes, an aging star might run
out of fuel. This causes the center
of the star to collapse in on itself,
producing an explosion that
destroys the star.

Are we even asking the right questions?

As humans, we often think of everything in terms
of beginnings and endings. After all, our lives begin
when we are born and end when we die. We begin to
exist and then we cease to exist. This way of thinking about
life shapes the way that we view the universe around us and
the questions that we ask.

Scientific study, however, tells us the matter that we are made from doesn't
actually begin when we are born or disappear when we die—rather, it changes form.

So instead of asking what created the universe in the beginning, are there
different questions that we might pose? Should we be asking what form our universe
might have taken before it changed into the one we now recognize?

What are we made from?

One of the things that we know from studying space is that matter can be changed, but it can't be created or destroyed. We can see water, for example, changing its form from liquid, to gas (steam), to solid ice. Although it might seem hard to imagine, much of our bodies are actually water, made from combining two separate elements—hydrogen and oxygen. Incredibly, the hydrogen in our bodies was formed in the Big Bang and the oxygen was formed in supernovas, all of which happened over billions of years.

The symbol for water is H_2O. This means that one oxygen atom and two hydrogen atoms combine to make a water molecule.

Exploding stars

Without supernovas there wouldn't be any life on Earth! The colossal core reactions of the exploding stars create vital chemical elements, such as oxygen, which form all living things. These newly formed elements then shoot out across space as stardust, creating new stars, planets, and…us.

Stardust

So, we, like everything else in the universe, are actually made from endlessly recycled stardust. In fact, we are made of the same stardust atoms that could once have formed part of a dinosaur, or a shooting star, or almost anything else that has ever existed in our universe. Imagine having one or two T. rex molecules in your body right now!

65% OXYGEN

18.5% CARBON

9.5% HYDROGEN

3.2% NITROGEN

1.5% CALCIUM

2.3% OTHER ELEMENTS

This is how to make a human: combine hydrogen, oxygen, carbon, nitrogen, and calcium, throw in a pinch of several other elements, and add a spoonful of a mystery ingredient—one that enables us to ask the question, "What am I made from!"

Humans in nature

We humans are animals, and we are a part of nature.
So why have humans often acted in ways that damage nature?

If we watched another animal on this Earth destroying everything that it needs in order to live, we would probably think that it was not very intelligent. Or, if we had our homes and lives destroyed by a creature that was burning down our houses or poisoning our water, we would take action to stop that animal. And yet, those who are doing the most damage to our planet are humans.

So why do some humans seem to think that they are so much better than other animals, and above the nature that surrounds them! After all, we are all made of the same elements. We share the same planet, and we need this planet to be healthy in order to keep ourselves healthy, too. It doesn't really make a lot of sense, so why do humans destroy so much of nature!

Mother Nature

Throughout history, Mother Nature has been worshipped as a creator goddess across many cultures. In Chile, Mother Nature is known as Pachamama and is revered as a goddess by the Indigenous people of the Andes. Papahānaumoku is the Earth Mother God of the ancient Hawaiian people. She has the power to give life to, and heal, everything in nature. The ancient Greeks believed that before Gaia, the ancestral mother of all life, there was only chaos. Then Gaia created the first gods, known as Titans, as well as the Earth and everything on it. In Hinduism, Shakti is the Divine Mother who creates and protects new life. Neither male nor female, Shakti is considered to be the creator of all of nature.

Rights of Nature

We used to live in harmony with nature. It is possible for us to remember how to do this and learn to protect the natural world. A number of laws have been passed around the world giving natural forms, such as rivers and forests, similar protection to humans. Known as the Rights of Nature, these laws recognize that the rest of nature has a right to exist and thrive without being disrupted by human activity. The Earth has been here for over four billion years—far longer than humans. Nature does not need humans, but humans need nature. Shouldn't the rest of nature have the same right to be protected as humans!

Can we measure everything?

We know that we humans and all other things in the known universe are made from matter. And we also know that there are forces, light, and energy. We know these things are there because we have studied them, learned how to measure them, and we know what form they take. But what about the things that we can't measure! How would you measure laughter, feelings, kindness, love, and friendship! Or ideas, thoughts, and fairness! If everything in the universe is made from the things that science knows, surely thoughts and feelings must also be made from these things!

If our thoughts and feelings have electrical energy, could it be possible for people to sense past events as a form of energy!

If we knew more about our thoughts and feelings, could we think more interesting thoughts and help ourselves feel better more of the time!

LAUGHTER KINDNESS IDEAS FRIENDSHIP FEELINGS

So, are these thoughts and feelings chemical reactions, or energy waves, or something else altogether? Are we walking, talking test tubes, fizzing with chemical reactions that make us behave in certain ways? Maybe we are actually controlled by the enormous quantities of bacteria that make up our bodies. Or is there, as many religious people believe, something more—a spirit or soul that inhabits our physical being?

The study of the human brain, called neuroscience, is still in its early stages. The more we study the brain, the more that we are able to see how different brain parts are activated when using particular thoughts or emotions. This suggests that these processes are chemical, but can they explain why we become best friends with one person and not another? As we delve deeper, who knows what we might discover as our knowledge and understanding of brain function develops!

Is learning about thoughts and feelings at school just as important as learning about math or spelling!

FAIRNESS

THOUGHTS

LOVE

V

10.0

20

50

Mapping the deep

What else lies at the bottom of the sea...and should we be looking?

To research the film *Avatar*, Canadian film director James Cameron built the submersible *Deepsea Challenger* so he could explore the bottom of the Mariana Trench.

The Mariana Trench is around 2 miles (3 km) deeper than Mount Everest is tall!

Strange creatures inhabit our deep seas and oceans. Each one of their unusual features has developed over thousands of years to increase their chance of survival in this dark, cold environment. Humans, however, have not evolved to survive there. This is one of the things that makes deep-sea exploration such a challenge.

Ocean water covers around 70 percent of the Earth's surface, provides most of the oxygen we breathe, food for billions of people, and regulates our climate by absorbing heat from the sun. The ocean floor is also rich in minerals and fossil fuels.

A place called Challenger Deep, in the Mariana Trench, is the deepest-known point on the planet. It lies around 36,000 ft (11,000 m) below the surface of the Pacific Ocean. So far, only 23 people have ever reached it.

Deep water exerts huge pressure on everything in it. Going thousands of feet down to the bottom of the ocean would expose humans to forces so strong that they would be crushed to death. So, currently, most of the research that is carried out on the ocean floor is done by unmanned vehicles, much like in space.

Many marine biologists and other experts are working tirelessly to protect the delicate ocean environment from human impact. But, if big companies travel down just to make more money by mining for materials, would it be better if the ocean floor wasn't explored? Could staying away from it be the best way to protect it?

Could you be a time traveler?

If you could invent a time machine, where and when would you travel to, and what would you do when you got there?

Draw out a timeline on a piece of paper, starting from the beginning of time and finishing at the end. Draw a dot where you are now, and a dot where you would like to go to. Fold the paper over, so the two dots are touching, and stick your pencil through them both. The hole that you have made is like a wormhole, connecting two places in time and space together.

Even though the time between your two dots could span hundreds or thousands of years, this wormhole creates a shortcut between these two points. Scientists and mathematicians have come up with a theory that wormholes could act like a gateway, or portal, allowing us to leap between different times. The only problem now is that we need more advanced technology to travel through the wormholes.

The Grandfather Paradox

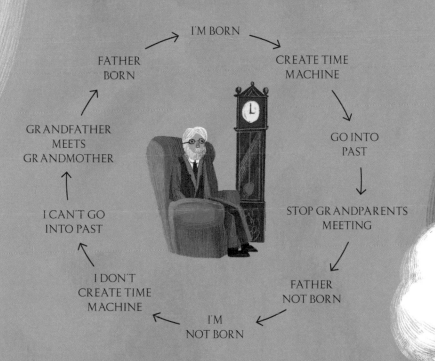

FATHER BORN → I'M BORN → CREATE TIME MACHINE

GRANDFATHER MEETS GRANDMOTHER

GO INTO PAST

I CAN'T GO INTO PAST

STOP GRANDPARENTS MEETING

I DON'T CREATE TIME MACHINE

I'M NOT BORN

FATHER NOT BORN

There are difficulties surrounding the possibility of time travel. One thought problem is the Grandfather Paradox: What would happen if you went back in time and stopped your grandfather from meeting your grandmother? If this happened, your mother or father wouldn't have been born, so you wouldn't have been born, so you couldn't go back and stop your grandparents from meeting. But then your grandparents would have met, and you would be born. This loop goes on with no answer, which makes it a paradox.

Parallel universes

In one version of the parallel universe idea, there are an infinite number of universes. Each time you make a decision in this universe, there could be an infinite number of "yourselves" making different decisions in other universes. So, next time you can't decide which ice cream flavor to choose, don't worry too much. The alternate "yous" might be choosing all the other flavors somewhere out there!

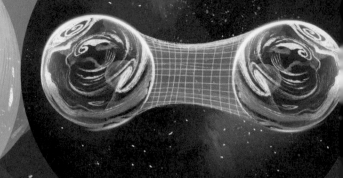

Is this the only universe?

Presently, we can only observe our own amazing universe—brimming full of stars, galaxies, black holes, and supernovas. However, ideas abound about the possibility of there being another, or even many other, universes out there.

Mirror universe

This theory puts forward the possible existence of a mirror universe, created at the moment of the Big Bang. However, in this mirror universe, everything is topsy-turvy— right is left, negative is positive, up is down, and time travels backward. It may sound like something out of a fantasy story, but who knows if this might not be true!

Universe bubbles

Next time you are sitting in a bubble bath, imagine that inside each one of those bubbles exists an entire universe. Then, watch the way that those bubbles bump into one another, join together, or split into two. This is another of the ideas suggested for possible multiverses. Could it be that there were many Big Bangs, just like the one that created our universe, creating many more universes, each one in its own bubble!

At the moment, explorations into multiverse theory are still at the thought–experiment stage. We can create models for the possible existence of other universes through exploring ideas around physics and math, but it still doesn't prove that these other universes exist.

Multiverse theory

The theory that there could be many universes is called multiverse theory. It looks at ideas around whether it is possible for other universes to coexist alongside our own, and what form they might take if they do. It explores the possibility that the universe that you are living in could turn out to be just a fragment of a much grander **MULTIVERSE!**

Glossary

ABORIGINAL Indigenous people of Australia

AFTERLIFE life or state of being that some people believe happens after death

ANCESTOR person from whom someone is descended, such as a great-great-grandmother

ARTIFICIAL INTELLIGENCE (AI) ability of machines or computers to behave and complete tasks in a similar way to humans

ASSASSINATION killing of an important person, such as a head of state, religious leader, or politician

ASTROBIOLOGY branch of biology that studies the possibility of life existing elsewhere in the universe

ASTROLOGY study of the movements and relative positions of the stars and other celestial bodies interpreted as having an influence on humans and the natural world

AVATAR image representation of a person that appears on a screen

CASTAWAY person who is stranded on a desert island after being shipwrecked

CAULDRON large, round, metal pot used for cooking over a fire and used by witches, wizards, and other practioners of magic for their spells

CELESTIAL something in the sky or heavens

CHARM magic spell or object containing the power to protect someone from evil or create good

CHEMICAL REACTION change that occurs to substances as a result of interacting with other substances

CLAIRVOYANT person believed to know about events in the future and to be able to communicate with the dead

COLOSSAL something that is extraordinarily large in size

CONCOCTION mixture of things

CONSPIRACY THEORY belief, usually unfounded, that a group of people are secretly trying to harm someone or achieve something

CONSTELLATION group of stars that create a pattern

CULTURE customs and beliefs of a particular group of people

CURSE particular type of spell designed to cause unpleasant things to happen to someone

DEMON devilish creature or spirit that seeks to do evil

DISEMBODIED separated from or existing without the body

DREAMTIME period of time in the Australian Aboriginal religion when powerful spirits created life and shaped the land into the form seen today

EERIE strange and frightening

ELEMENTS different parts of the atmosphere of planet Earth that make up the weather

EXTRASENSORY PERCEPTION (ESP) being aware of something without use of the five senses, such as hearing

FANTASY story that is based on imagination and not on reality

FOLKLORE traditional beliefs, stories, or customs of a community of people

FRAUDULENT action carried out deliberately designed to deceive

GOD supernatural being worshipped for having great powers and who sometimes influences human events

GRAVITY force that causes things to fall to the ground

GUARDIAN magical spirit that provides care to people who believe in it

HABITABLE conditions that provide enough comfort for people or animals to live

HALLUCINATION seeing something that isn't actually there because of illness or an illusion

HOAX believable trick or lie that is ultimately untrue

INANIMATE lacking any sign of life

INCENSE substance that is burned for its distinct smell, sometimes as part of a religious ritual

INFINITY never-ending point in space and time, and an ever-increasing number that has no mathematical value

JINN type of spirit from Arabic mythology that can take on many forms; also called a genie

LEGEND mythical story from the past telling of a famous deed or action

MAGICIAN person who is a practitioner or performer of magic

MARINE relating to animals and plants that live in the sea

MARTIAN life thought to have come from the planet Mars

MATTER particular type of substance, usually solid, liquid, or gas

MEDIEVAL people, places, things, and events of the Middle Ages

MICROSCOPIC extremely small objects that can usually only be seen through a microscope

MIDDLE AGES period of time covering the years between 476 CE to around 1500

MINERAL naturally occurring substance that can be found in rocks and the earth, but which is not living

MIRAGE something that is seen and appears to be real but does not actually exist

MYTH/MYTHOLOGY ancient stories from a single culture that collectively explain the legendary history of that group, often explaining the nature of the world, and often including supernatural characters

NATIVE AMERICAN relating to the Indigenous peoples of North and South America, especially in the area of the USA and Canada, who first settled on the land

NORSE people and lands of ancient Scandinavia, including areas conquered by the Vikings, such as Greenland

PHANTOM ghost or spirit

PHILOSOPHICAL relating to the study of knowledge, reality, and the important issues in life

POISON dangerous substance that can kill or harm a person or animal if swallowed or absorbed

PORTAL gateway or entrance to another place

POTION liquid that contains ingredients making it either magical, poisonous, or filled with healing qualities

POULTICE piece of cloth covered with a thick, often warm substance, wrapped around an injury to ease pain or swelling

PROPHECY prediction concerning a future event

PROWESS demonstration of great ability and skill doing a particular thing

PSYCHIC ability to read another person's mind and possibly communicate with the dead

RADAR use of radio signals to discover the position or speed of objects, such as aircraft or ships

REMEDY substance that provides a cure to illness or harm

RITUAL ceremony carried out in a certain way, usually due to traditional or religious reasons

RUNES letters of an ancient language, such as Norse

SACRED item, idea, or place believed to have special religious importance

SALVE ointment used to protect or heal the skin

SEANCE meeting where people gather and try to communicate with the dead

SIXTH SENSE instinctive awareness of something without using the five senses of sight, smell, hearing, touch, and taste

SONAR system that uses sound waves to calculate the depth of the sea or the position of an underwater object

SORCERY magic performed, usually with evil intentions

SPECTER spirit or ghost with evil intent

SPELL controlling or affecting a person or situation through the use of magical power

SPIRIT ghost or magical being without physical form; also the soul of a person

SUBTERRANEAN area existing below the surface of the Earth

SUPERNATURAL relating to actions or forces that go beyond the recognized laws of nature

SURVEILLANCE closely watching someone or something in order to obtain information about them

SYMBOL something that represents or stands for something else

TELEPATHY communication of thoughts and feelings between people's minds without expressing them through the senses

TRANSPARENT object or substance that is completely see-through

UFO unidentified flying object of unknown origin that is often thought to be from another planet

UNCONSCIOUS part of your mind that contains feelings and ideas that you do not know about or cannot control

UNDERWORLD mythical land of the dead, imagined to be under the ground

VISION seeing something or someone that other people are unable to

Index

Senior Editor Marie Greenwood
Designer Brandie Tully-Scott
US Senior Editor Shannon Beatty
US Editor Mindy Fichter
Acquisitions Editor James Mitchem
Managing Editor Jonathan Melmoth
Managing Art Editor Diane Peyton Jones
Jacket Coordinator Magda Pszuk
Senior Production Editor Nikoleta Parasaki
Production Controller Magdalena Bojko
Publishing Director Sarah Larter
Authenticity Consultant Bianca Hezekiah

First American Edition, 2023
Published in the United States by DK Publishing
1745 Broadway, 20th Floor, New York, NY 10019

Copyright © 2023 Dorling Kindersley Limited
Text copyright © 2023 Tamara Macfarlane
DK, a Division of Penguin Random House LLC
23 24 25 26 27 10 9 8 7 6 5 4 3 2 1
001–334928–Sep/2023

Published in Great Britain by Dorling Kindersley Limited
A catalog record for this book
is available from the Library of Congress.
ISBN 978-0-7440-8052-0
DK books are available at special discounts when purchased
in bulk for sales promotions, premiums, fund-raising, or
educational use. For details, contact:
DK Publishing Special Markets,
1745 Broadway, 20th Floor, New York, NY 10019
SpecialSales@dk.com

Printed and bound in China

For the curious
www.dk.com

MIX
Paper | Supporting
responsible forestry
FSC® C018179

This book was made with Forest
Stewardship Council™ certified
paper—one small step in DK's
commitment to a sustainable future.
**For more information go to
www.dk.com/our-green-pledge**

FOR L AND X AND ALL THE MAGIC THEY BRING

Acknowledgments

The author would like to give a huge thanks to:
Marie, James, Brandie, Kristina Kister, and the whole
DK team for making this book such an unending joy to
work on; and to Roy, Neil, and Tai for all their support,
advice, and endless tea and coffee.

DK would like to thank: Kieran Jones and Abi Maxwell
for additional editorial help; Polly Goodman for
proofreading; Helen Peters for the index.

✦ ✦ ───────────────────────◖

About the author,
Tamara Macfarlane

Tamara Macfarlane is a children's author and founder
of Moon Lane Children's Books, which includes
the award-winning *Tales on Moon Lane*. As
a child, Tamara escaped to Blackwell's children's
bookshop in Oxford at every opportunity and would
have lived there if she had been allowed. Happily
blurring the lines between reality and reading led her
to Arthur C. Clarke and his work on the unexplained.
A fascination that bordered on obsession began.

✦ ✦ ───────────────────────◖

From the illustrator,
Kristina Kister

I am an illustrator from Essen, Germany. After
graduating in communication design and working at
an advertising agency, I became a full-time children's
book illustrator. When I emigrated from Russia to
Germany as a child, all I had with me were two books
about everything mysterious and magical. These books
played an important part in how I see the world today.
That is why I am really excited to work on this book,
because it reminds me of my childhood and I know
that I would have absolutely loved this book.